Peter's Name

FR. TELESPHOR SMYTH-VAUDRY

NIHIL OBSTAT.

JOANNES PINNEL,
Censor deputatus.

IMPRIMATUR.

† JOANNES ANTONIUS,
Ep. Sti. Antonii.

In festo Cathedrae S. Petri Romae, A. D. 1909.

GENERAL DIVISIONS

First Part,—

Peter's name proclaims him **possessor** of all Church-power, under Christ.

Second Part,—

Peter's name proclaims him the **source** of all Church-power, under Christ.

Table of Contents

FIRST PART

SECOND PART

First Part

Peter's Name Proclaims Him

POSSESSOR

of all Church-power, Under Christ

First Part

Peter's name proclaims him *possessor* of all Church-power, under Christ.

(By Church-power we understand the threefold power vested in the Church by our divine Lord, viz., the ruling, teaching, and sanctifying power: the royal, prophetic, and sacerdotal office.)

NOTE I

Peter's name means, scripturally, Christ's other self

A startling similarity

In our notes on the Names of Jesus and Peter in Holy Writ, we have seen that these two names, by reason of the startling similarity of treatment which they receive in the Scriptures, forcibly suggest a corresponding similarity or identity of office in their respective bearers. In fact, the Word of God affirms such identity of office (viz., the papal office) in Jesus and Peter, by applying the papal title of the Rock to the Master as well as to His Chief Apostle: Matt. 7. 24; 16. 18; John 1. 42; 1 Cor. 10. 4.

Let us glance, once more, at the marvelous similarity of treatment and the sovereign pre-eminence bestowed by Holy Writ on the names of Jesus and Peter.

(a) The New Testament invariably ranges the Apostles under Jesus in its every mention of them in connection with the Master.

The New Testament likewise systematically ranges all the Apostles under Peter in its four catalogs of the Apostles, and in its every mention by name of a fraction or group of the Apostolic College in connection with him.

(b) The New Testament groups the Apostles even anonymously under the head-name of Jesus.

In precisely the same manner, does it group the Apostles even anonymously under the head-name of Peter as the future or actual successor of Christ in the visible headship of the Church—thus putting Peter on a relative level of authority with Christ Himself not only by ranging all under him but by suppressing all names except Christ's and Peter's.

(c) The New Testament makes more frequent mention of Jesus by name than of all the Apostles and disciples.

The new Testament likewise makes more frequent mention of, and consequently devotes more attention to, Peter,—by name, singly and individually—than to any other Apostle, not excepting St. Paul and the two other leading Apostles, St. John and St. James.

In short, the names of Jesus and Peter hold the first, the most conspicuous and the most commanding position in Holy Writ.

A Triple Scale of ever-ascending grandeur

It is now our purpose, in this series of Notes, to take a closer view of the scriptural meaning and import of the name of Peter.

It is a name which is very far from receiving its due meed of praise and admiration. Who ever adverts to its triple force and import? For, Peter's name is a triple scale of ever ascending grandeur—a triple firmament superposed one over the other and rising up to heights which angel wings can never mount.

First, it alone is scripturally, and all in one, a title of office, a personal proper name, and a God-given name.

Second, it alone is scripturally and all in one, a title of office, a personal proper name, a God-given name, and a Divine name besides—i. e., one of God's own scriptural names and titles.

Third, it is a name which God shares with none, except Christ and Simon Barjona—to the exclusion of all the rest of creation.

(First) Peter's name alone is scripturally, and all in one, a title of office, a personal proper name, and a God-given name.

It is a God-given name; not conferred by an Angel, like Israel's (Gen. 32. 28), or by a prophet, but by the Lord Incarnate in person: (John 1. 42; Mark 3. 16.)

The surname of Boanerges was indeed conferred on James and John by our Lord himself (Mark 3. 17). —not however as an essential, but as a purely incidental, addition to their names. It was not a substitute for the same. Much less was it a title of office. Hence, they are, ever after, designated in Holy Writ as James and John, never under the appellation of Boanerges.

But Peter's name was given him both as an essential and perpetual addition to, and substitute for, that of Simon Barjona, and as an essential perpetual title of office. Therefore does Holy Writ almost constantly call him by that Divine name— over one hundred and sixty times.

Note again that Abraham's name, though God-given (Gen. 17. 5) is not, like Peter's, a Divine title of office.

Peter, then, it may be objected, was more favored of heaven, in one respect at least, than Jesus Himself —since Jesus received his name through the ministry of an angel (Matt. 1. 21; Luke 1. 31). The answer suggests itself at once, that, if Jesus did, outwardly, receive his name through an angel, He received it inwardly, in the sanctuary of his soul,—not only directly but with infinite directness, from the Father—in the threefold embrace of his eternal generation, of his temporal filiation, and of the face-to-face vision.

(Second) Peter's name alone is scripturally, and all in one, a title of office, a personal proper name, a God-given name and a Divine name besides,—it being one of God's own scriptural names and titles.

No such distinction attaches to the names of Abraham and Boanerges. They are God-given, but they are not God's own personal names and titles.

True, God has been pleased to share some of his own scriptural names with men and with the heavenly spirits above. With myriads of the latter, for instance, does he share the beautiful title of Angel; for, He calls himself the Angel, the Angel of the Covenant: Mal. 3. 1; Matt. 11. 10; Mark 1. 2; Luke 1. 76; and 7. 27.

The Creator shares his very name of God with us, as an earnest of eternal glory as well as of the super-human, super-angelic, divine nature and dignity which we receive in baptism. Thus, for instance, speaketh the Lord to his deified children, in the book of Psalms: "I have said, Ye are gods and all of you the sons of the Most High:" Psalm 81. 6; John 10. 34.

He also shares with us His title of Father, as a title of love. "For this cause," says St. Paul, "I bow my knees to the Father of our Lord Jesus Christ, of whom all paternity in heaven and earth is named." Eph. 3. 15.

We should, however, carefully note that God does not bestow these names of His—Angel, God, Father —upon any creature as *proper* individual names, but only as *common* names or titles either of office, or of honor.

On the other hand, Peter's name, which is one of God's own names and titles, has been conferred upon Simon Barjona not only as Simon's Divine title of office but as Simon's own perpetual proper name. Now, to no other mere creature has God said, as He did virtually to Peter: "Behold, one of my own personal names shall be thine own individual proper name."

For, remember that the Holy Spirit gives the name of Rock or Peter—to Jehovah, to the Redeemer and

Saviour, to the Christ, to God Incarnate and manifest in the flesh, and finally to Simon Barjona.

----

a. The Holy Spirit calls Jehovah "Rock," i. e., Peter.

And note, in this connection, that, according to the divine tradition of the old Synagogue, the name "Jehovah," considered as a unit, signifies the absolute oneness of God—whilst, viewed in its four component Hebrew letters, it signifies God the Father, the Son, the Holy Ghost, and God Incarnate. Therefore, in applying the name of Rock to Jehovah, the Holy Spirit applies it to the blessed Trinity and to the sacred Humanity of the Redeemer. (See our Notes on the Church and the Synagogue.)

The Holy Spirit calls Jehovah "Rock," or Peter, for instance, in Deut. 32. 4: "Ascribe ye greatness unto our God, the Rock."

1 Sam. 2. 2: Neither is there any rock like our God.

1 Sam. 23. 3: The God of Israel said, the Rock of Israel spake—.

Ps. 17. 2, 31: Jehovah is my Rock and my fortress.... Who is a rock, save our God?

Ps. 29. 1: Unto thee will I cry, O Jehovah, my Rock.

Ps. 72. 26: God is the Rock of my heart.

Is. 26. 4: Trust ye in the Lord forever: for in the Lord Jehovah is the Rock of ages.

----

b. THE HOLY SPIRIT GIVES THE NAME OF ROCK OR PETER TO THE REDEEMER AND SAVIOUR: for instance, in Gen. 49. 24: And the arms of his hands were made strong by the hands of the Mighty One of Jacob —from thence is the Shepherd, the (Stone or) Rock of Israel.

Deut. 32. 15: Then he forsook God who made him, and lightly esteemed the Rock of his salvation.

2 Sam. 22. 47. Jehovah liveth, and blessed be my Rock; and exalted be the God of the Rock of my salvation.

Ps. 18. 15. O Jehovah, my Rock and my Redeemer!

P. 88. 27: Rock of my salvation.

Ps. 94. 1: Make a joyful noise to the Rock of our salvation.

Note, in connection with Gen. 49. 24, "from thence is the Shepherd, the Rock of Israel," that Messiah calls himself the Good Shepherd (John 10. 14) and the Rock: Matt. 7. 24; and 21. 42.

———

c. THE HOLY SPIRIT GIVES THE NAME OF ROCK, OR PETER, TO THE CHRIST—for instance, in 1 Cor. 10. 4: For they drank of that spiritual Rock that followed them, and that Rock was Christ.

———

d. THE HOLY SPIRIT GIVES THE NAME OF ROCK, OR PETER, TO GOD INCARNATE and manifest in the flesh —for instance, in Matt. 7. 24, our Lord praises the wisdom of the man who builds his house on the Rock, i. e., on the Christ himself.

God Incarnate and manifest in the flesh calls Himself the Rock or the Stone, in Matt. 7. 24; 21. 42; 21. 44; Luke 20. 17, 18. See also Acts. 4. 11; Eph. 2. 20; 1. Pet. 2. 4, 6, 7, 8. —

Many centuries before His advent, THE SYNAGOGUE HERSELF HAILED MESSIAH AS THE ROCK and as Jehovah, thereby proclaiming him God by nature and by essence; for, such is the rabbinical as well as the biblical import of the term "Jehovah." We could multiply citations from authorised Jewish sources, but our limited space restricts us to a few.

Medrasch-Rabba on Lamentations, fol. 68, col. 2, ed. Amsterdam—says: "What is the name of Messiah? Rabbi Abba, son of Cahana, answers: Jehovah is his Name."

Through Rabbi Solomon Yarhhi, the Synagogue teaches that "the Rock is King Messiah." (On. Is. 28. 16.)

The same Rabbi sums up the witness of the ancient Fathers of the Synagogue in the following sentence, which he puts in the mouth of Jehovah: "I am he who has laid that foundation (Is. 28. 16). From of old have I resolved this thing, and I have raised King Messiah to be in Sion a tried stone," or rock. (Drach: Harmonie entre l'Eglise et la Synagogue, vol. 2, p. 421.)

How beautiful the prayer of the Synagogue through the royal prophet David: "O Jehovah, my Rock and my Redeemer" (Ps. 18. 15).—It is a cry of infinite yearning that rends the heavens and haunts the ages.

How pathetic the testimony of the Synagogue through one of her sons, the well-known Jewish writer Philo. Listen to words of profound sublimity, echoing the purest traditions of the old Jewish Church of God. Philo (B. C. 30) writes:—"The law-giver says: 'Jehovah hath made His people suck honey out of the rock and oil out of the hardest rock.' (Deut. 32. 13)— the solid Rock, the indissoluble Rock that none can break. Moses designates, by that Rock, the *Wisdom* of God, who tenderly feedeth, nurseth and reareth those who aspire to the incorruptible life. This Rock, become as it were the mother of all men in the world, presents to her children *a food which she draws from her own substance*... But all are not found worthy of that Divine food... The inspired writer, employing somewhere else an equivalent expression, calls that Rock MANNA, *The Divine Word more ancient than all beings.*" "The Rock is King Messiah," says the Synagogue. (See our Notes on the Church and the Synagogue, pp. 78, 106, etc.—and Drach's Harmonie entre l'Eglise et la Synagogue, 2d. vol. pp. 395, 477— 478, etc.)

(Third) Rock, or Peter, is a name of God which He shares with none except Christ and Simon Barjona, to the exclusion of all the rest of creation.

So jealous is Jehovah of the name and title of Rock that He will not share it with any being in heaven and on earth, except Jesus Christ and Peter.

Holy Writ indeed compares Abraham to a quarry or rock, but confers *not* that name upon him. The term is simply applied to him by way of comparison, *not* as a proper name. His first name, Abram, was changed into Abraham, not into Peter. His title was Father of a multitude, not the Rock, not Cephas.

Inasmuch as Christ's person pertains to the Godhead, *Peter is the one and sole personality in all creation with whom God shares His name and title of Rock.* As a human person, Peter alone among all the sons of Adam, Peter alone, Peter continued in his succession, enjoys such a unique prerogative.

Behold a wonder of surpassing magnitude and significance: Jehovah proclaims Jesus Christ, "Rock," or "Peter," and He proclaims Simon, "Rock," or Peter."

What a divine proclamation of Simon Barjona's office as Christ's "other self" (St. Augustin): Jehovah-the-Rock, Jesus-the-Rock, Christ-the-Rock, and Simon-the-Rock!

What a truly divine proclamation of a truly divine office! Hear: Jehovah-Peter, Jesus-Peter, Christ-Peter, and Simon-Peter!

Christ Jesus is the vicarious Rock of Jehovah, and Peter is the vicarious Rock of God Incarnate—Christ's "other self," says St. Augustin: Serm. 46.

(See our Notes on the Names of Jesus and Peter in Holy Writ, page 10, etc.)

"Thou art Peter (or Rock) and upon this Rock I will build My Church" Matt. 16. 18.

Beza, the heresiarch, who calls the pope "Antichrist," is compelled to say of our text:

"The Lord speaking in Syriac .... said Kepha in both places:"— i. e., our Lord said, "Thou art Kepha and upon this Kepha I will build my Church: Thou art Rock and upon this Rock I will build my Church."

Of the Greek translation of this same passage of S. Matthew, Beza says: "In Greek likewise, petros and petra differ only in their termination, *not* in their meaning:"— i. e., in Greek as well as in Syriac the meaning is: "Thou art Rock and upon this Rock I will build my Church." (Cfr. C. à Lap. in loco.)

"The writer of the Greek simply gave to the term, when used as a surname of Simon, a masculine ending [Petr-*os*] for the sake of the grace of language, since both terms mean a rock." (Breen.)

The ripest Protestant scholarship holds with Dr. Briggs, of the Protestant Episcopal Church, that "all attempts to explain the Rock in any other way but as referring to Peter have ignominiously failed." (North Amer. Rev., Feb. 15, 1907.)

Another Protestant writer, Dr. Marsh, rightly remarks: "It seems a *desperate* undertaking to prove that our Saviour alluded to any other person than to St. Peter, for the words of the passage can indicate no one else." (Comparative View, app. n. D.)—

A third Protestant divine, Rev. J. S. Thompson, is not less emphatic: "Protestants.... have used all the hardihood of *lawless* criticism in their attempts to reason away the Catholic interpretation." (Monotessaron, p. 194, Baltimore, 1829: ap. Brandi's Why am I a Catholic.)

NOTE II

—

Peter's name is the scriptural equivalent of the Catholic term "Pope"

We can never lay too much stress on a fact of incalculable importance, which is quite commonly overlooked and neglected: the fact that, both in its scriptural and in its traditional meaning, the term "Peter" is the exact equivalent of the Catholic term "Pope."

Simon Peter, as a compound name, meant from the first with the Apostles and their followers—Simon the Rock, Simon the Head, Simon the Confirmer of the Faith, the Supreme Ruler, the Vicegerent of Jesus Christ—in a word, Simon the Pope, as we would say now-a-days.

We have frequently adverted to this beautiful and prolific truth; but it is inexhaustible and susceptible of additional proof.

As "Jesus" is not merely a personal name but a title of office, so "Peter" is not merely the name of a person otherwise called Simon; it is moreover a momentous title of office. As the name of Jesus is expressive, declarative and commemorative of the Messiahship of Christ, and means literally and really "the Saviour:" so, by the express will of Christ, the name of Peter is expressive, declarative and commemorative of the headship of Simon, and means Simon the Rock, the Head, the Supreme Ruler. It is the name of the very office of Christ given to Peter to indicate that Peter inherits the office of the Master. Christ invests Peter with his own glorious title of "Rock," the better to show that Peter is Christ's other self, to use once more the language of St. Augustin.

Jesus says to Simon, not in so many words, but by clear implication: "What more can I do, O Simon, to proclaim my solemn appointment of thee as my successor in office? Behold, as some of the kings of the earth who have the good of their kingdom at heart most wisely crown their successors with their own hand before departing from this life—so do I now myself crown thee as my successor before I lay down my life for my beloved kingdom. Yea, as some of the crowned heads of this world put their crown upon the brow of their intended successor—so do I now put on thy brow, O Simon, more than a diadem: I crown thee with my own royal name and title of office, the most momentous name and title in the sphere of Church-government, after that of Jesus. Therefore, even as I am the Rock or Cephas the First, or Peter the First—so do I appoint thee Cephas or Peter the Second; mark, Peter the Second, *not* Peter the last. For, as thou art my official self visibly continued, so wilt thou thyself be officially and visibly continued in thy succession which, being, as thou art, the foundation of the Church, must needs last as long as the Church in order to protect her from the gates of hell.

I am the one Foundation, and thou, O Peter, art no other foundation indeed, but the visible force, the visible effluence, the visible continance of the one Foundation.

I am the Rock by nature and by right, whilst thou, O Peter, art the Rock by participation and by grace.

Thou shalt bear my name, as being personally incorporated into my own royal dynasty and the *visible* continuance thereof. My Apostles and disciples must revere thee as such, thy very *name* being to them all a perpetual reminder of thy divine vicegerency."

Now, the Apostles and the disciples knew that Christ's strictly personal office, as the Redeemer of the world and the Founder of Christianity and the author of its doctrines, sacraments and essential polity—was absolutely untransferable, such transference being, moreover, uncalled for and unnecessary. But they also knew, from the very name of Peter, that Christ's visible office as the Rock goes with the bearer of the name of the Rock and must needs continue here below; for, without such a Rock (Christ avers) his Church would collapse under the powers or gates of hell, Matt. 16. 18: i. e., falsehood or heresy, and internal disruption or schism.

Peter's name, then, tells the Apostles and the Church, with *Christ's own lips,* as it were, that Peter has inherited the threefold office of the Rock: that he is the Rock of Authority, the Rock of infallible Truth and the Rock of the legitimate Priesthood—the Rock of authority that binds and keeps the Church in the indivisible unity of the one compact mystic Body of Jesus Christ. Eph. 4. 16;

Peter is the Rock of authority: for, he is the Foundation, and as the whole structure follows the foundation, so does the whole Church follow Peter as her Christ-appointed ruler.

Peter is the Rock of infallible Truth that binds and keeps the Church in the indivisible unity of the one Faith or doctrine of Jesus Christ, Eph. 4. 5; the Rock or sacrificial Stone of the one legitimate Priesthood, that binds and keeps the Church in the indivisible unity of sacrificial worship and sacramental communion in Jesus Christ. Eph. 4. 5.

Yes, Peter is the Rock of the priesthood: for Christ founded on Peter his *whole* Church—apostolate and priesthood and laity. Therefore, a priesthood severed from the foundation (Peter), is out of the Christ-established order—is unlawful and illegitimate.

Christ's other self, supreme ruler, infallible teacher, sovereign pontiff holding the visible place and office of Jesus Christ over the Church: such is the scriptural face-value and face-meaning of the name of Peter.

Even the Synagogue, though prophetically and historically a mere preparatory school for the universal or Catholic Church, was nevertheless endowed with an infallible oracle in her sovereign Pontificate. Was the type better equipped than the reality? Was the shadow more solid than the substance? Was a purely local and national organism better safeguarded against error and division than the world-embracing organisation founded by God Incarnate in Person?

NOTE III

Peter's name means, scripturally, the sovereign Ruler, infallible Teacher, and High Priest of the Church.

That our Lord himself wrote on the very face of Peter's name the Divine proof of its bearer's supremacy, is evident from the text itself and from the scriptural explanation vouchsafed by the Master of Wisdom (first) on the occasion of the bestowal of the name, and (second) on subsequent occasions.

(a) Our Lord explains to his Apostles the original and divine meaning of the name of Peter as signifying (Matt. 16. 19.) the Key-bearer-in-chief of the Kingdom of God on earth, whose binding and loosing power is independent and supreme—it being conceded to him singly, individually and independently, whilst it is only later on conceded to the other Apostles collectively, and by consequence, limitedly, in perfect subordination to the visible head under whom our Lord had already placed them.

(b) Again, our Lord explains the original and divine meaning of the name of Peter as signifying (Luke 22. 31) the Confirmer of the Brethren—of all the Brethren without restriction or exception—the Confirmer of the whole Church, the Confirmer whose Faith can never fail because Christ has prayed to that effect, and His prayer cannot remain unheard (John 11. 42).

(c) Our Lord explains the original and divine meaning of the name of Peter as signifying (John 21.

15—17) the Pastor of the lambs and of the sheep, i. e., the infallible Guide and supreme Ruler of the whole flock.

All the above explanations are obviously included in the Petrine name and the accompanying text itself, and are regarded in that light by all ancient commentators.

In short, the very name of Peter was conferred of set purpose by our Lord as being in itself, and by itself alone, both the best reminder and the most obvious proof of Peter's divine commission and office as the Christ or the Rock officially continued as supreme ruler, infallible teacher and sovereign pontiff of the Christian brotherhood.

Infallibility.

A glance at the central Petrine text will suffice to convince the reader.

"And I say to thee: that thou art Rock and upon this Rock I will build my Church, and the gates of hell shall not prevail against it:" Matt. 16. 18.

Our Lord begins by reminding his hearers of the essential veracity of Him who addresses them: "And *I* say to thee"—i. e., I, who am Truth itself (John 14. 6)—I, who am the Eternal Word of God (John 1. 1) —I, whose word shall abide whilst heaven and earth shall pass away (Matt. 24. 35)—I say that *my* Church shall be built on Peter.

Therefore, according to our Lord, His Church has no existence outside of Peter. Or, to put our Lord's teaching in a still more intelligible form, out of Peter there is no Church of Christ and, consequently, no salvation. Every church not built on Peter shall fall a prey to the powers of hell.

Now, a living and divine Foundation out of which there can be no divine Church, no "pillar and ground of the truth" (1 Tim. 3. 15)—a living and divine Foundation which, according to the Lord's promise, shall ever prevent the gates of hell from prevailing against the Church, i. e., from seducing her into heresy, schism, and apostasy—such a living and divine Foundadation (it is evident) must of necessity be an infallible Guide to heaven. Else we would have the monstrous anomaly of an infallible Church built on a fallible foundation and yet vitally inseparable therefrom. Or, —in the hypothesis of a fallible Church built on an equally fallible foundation,—if the Foundation which our Lord Himself declares essentially inseparable from *His* Church, is at the same time officially fallible and liable to err—then it follows that the divine Church must, willing or nilling, cling to a false and misleading Foundation under pain of ceasing to be the Church of God and of being eternally lost!

Surely, the living and divine Foundation out of which there can be no Church of Christ and from which the Church is perpetually drawing her immunity from the destructive errors signified by the gates of hell—must be able to discern infallibly truth and error: else it would unwittingly lend itself to deceivers and would thus become the unconscious prop or inept abettor of falsehood, the prop of heresy and wickedness. Thus, the Christ-established Foundation would become the most dreadful underminer, dissolvent and disrupter of the very Church which it was divinely and explicitly intended to perpetuate.

Supremacy

It is not enough for the Foundation of the Church to be inerrant and infallible—i. e., to be able to distinguish between truth and error, between true and false teachers; in a word, between those who should and those who should not be allowed to rest in peace on the Rock of the Church. The living Foundation must, moreover, wield adequate authority on each and every member that claims its recognition, as implied in Church membership. The living Foundation must have direct and continuous control over the sheep as well as over the lambs, in order to eliminate the bad or dangerous and watch over the good members of the Flock.

Shorn of that adequate control over every member, the living Foundation becomes a mere stage-potentate, a solemn manikin, a King Log, and must passively lend itself to numberless heresy-breeders or schism-mongers, who would remain upon the unwilling Foundation in spite and in defiance of the Foundation itself, and could boldly reply to all opponents: "We are grounded on the Foundation of the Rock established by Christ Jesus, and we are therefore members of the Church—the express will of the living Foundation to the contrary notwithstanding!"

Thus left at the mercy of all heretics and schismatics, the Church would be compelled to harbor them all—compelled to foster a brood of serpents in her bosom and to die eventually the ignominious death of a moral suicide. In a word, shorn of infallibility, the living foundation would unwittingly lend its countenance to error; shorn of supremacy, the living Foundation would be compelled to lie ignominiously and groan helplessly (like the sects) under every form of error and falsehood. In either case, instead of being a boon and a blessing, the living Foundation would be "a scandal in your brother's way" (Rom. 14. 13)— instead of being a guiding light, it would be "a stumbling block.... before the blind:" (Levit. 19. 14.)

Therefore, either the living Foundation of the Church is a stumbling block and a scandal, or it is infallible in doctrine and supreme in authority.

And this is precisely the lesson which the word of God spells out in the *name* of Peter or Cephas

Peter is infallible: why? His very name tells you why, viz., because he is the Rock that can never be blown about, "tossed to and fro and carried about," like shifting sands, "by every wind of doctrine." Eph. 4. 14.

Peter is supreme Ruler: why? His very name tells you why, viz., because he is the Rock that makes the Church hell-proof and invincible (Matt. 16. 18) by the virtue and force he imparts to her members by means of his full adequate control and authority over each and every one of them.

Without the sceptre of supremacy how could he protect the Church against the gates of hell? How could he confirm, strengthen, compact together and energize a body whose members are exempt from and elude his beneficial control and sovereignty?

Therefore it is that Christ made His own fundamental office as teacher, ruler and priest, so absolutely inseparable from his successor Simon Peter, that He made it impossible to *name* Peter without naming, in the same word and in the same breath, the fundamental office bequeathed to the same august personage.

The East and the West unite in acknowledging that the Word of God proclaims, *in and through the name itself of Peter*, the latter's inheritance of Christ's divine office as the infallible guide and supreme Shepherd of the Fold.

———

NOTE IV

Scriptural meaning of Peter's name according to the Fathers

Scriptural meaning of Peter's name according to St. John Chrysostom:

"When I name Peter, I name that *unbroken Rock*, that *firm Foundation,* the great Apostle, *the First* of the Disciples." (Hom. de Poenitentia.)

"He that was really *Peter both in name and in deed.*" (Id. on text.)

"The support of the Faith." (Hom. on the Ten Thousand Talents.)

"The Leader of that Choir."—viz., the Apostolic College—"the Mouth of the Apostles, *the Head* of that Family, *the Governor of the whole world,* the Foundation of the Church." (Hom. in illud: Hoc scitote.)

"The basis of the Church." (Hom. in illud: Vidi Dominum.)

"The basis of the Faith." (Contra Lud. et theat.)

Speaking of the same blessed Apostle, St. Chrysostom still more emphatically remarks: "Christ inserted in *His name a guarantee* and a sign of solidity of Faith." (In illud: Paulus vocatus.)

Scriptural meaning of Peter's name according to Origen:

"That great Foundation of the Church and most solid Rock on which Christ founded His Church." (In Exod., Hom. 5. n. 4.)

According to the Council of Chalcedon (A. D. 451) "St. Peter is the Rock and foundation of the Catholic Church and the Basis of the orthodox Faith." (Act. 3 etc. in deposing Dioscorus.)

Scriptural meaning of Peter's name according to Sergius, Metropolitan of Cyprus, A. D. 643:

"*O holy Head*, Christ our God hath destined the Apostolic See to be an *immovable foundation*: *pillar of the Faith!* For, thou art, as the Divine Word truly said, Peter, and *on thee* as on a foundation-stone *have the pillars of the Church been fixed*." (Lat. 1, Sess. 2., Labbé t. 7., p. 125.)

Scriptural meaning of Peter's name according to St. Theodore of Studium, A. D. 826:

"*O Apostolic Head!* O Shepherd of the sheep of Christ set over them by God! O Door-Keeper of the Kingdom of Heaven! *O Rock of the Faith upon which the Catholic Church is built*: for Peter thou art."

According to St. Epiphanius 'Peter' means "the immovable Rock." (Haer. 59, n. 7.)

According to St. Gregory Nazianzen, 'Peter' means "the second Foundation from Christ." (In hom. archier. inserta.)

Scriptural meaning of Peter's name according to St. Ambrose:

"The Apostle in whom is the Church support"— i. e., against the gates of hell. (On Luke l. 4, n. 70.)

"Christ is the Rock, but yet He did not deny the grace of this name to His disciple that He should be

Peter, because he has from the Rock firm constancy, *immovable Faith."* (On Luke, l. 6, n. 97.)

Scriptural meaning of Peter's name according to ST. LEO THE GREAT, A. D. 461:

"For thou art Peter, that is, whereas I am the inviolable Rock; I the corner-stone who made both one; I the foundation besides which no one can lay another; yet thou also art a Rock, because thou art consolidated by my might, that what things alone are mine by mine power may be common to thee by participation with me." (Serm. 4 in Natal. Ordin., c. 2, ed. Ballerini.)

St. Leo tells us here that St. Peter's name means scripturally the Rock "by participation," the sharer, by participation, in "the things" that are Christ's in His own right—the sharer in Christ's fundamental office as sovereign ruler, and sovereign teacher, and sovereign pontiff of the Church.

Still more striking is the language of the saint in the following sentence:

"That which the Truth ordered remains: and blessed Peter, persisting in that strength of the Rock which he received, has not deserted the guidance, once undertaken, of the Church. For, thus was he set before the rest that while *he is called the Rock*—that is, while he is declared to be the Foundation; while he is appointed the Door-Keeper of the Kingdom of heaven; while he is promoted to be the Judge of what shall be bound and what loosed, with the assurance that his sentence shall be ratified even in heaven— *we might learn through the very mystery of the name given to him how he was associated with Christ."* (Serm. 3 on Anniv.)

It is with profound reason, therefore, that the Church reads in St. Peter's *name* a great object-lesson teaching his intimate association and co-partnership with Christ—he being Christ's visible associate and co-adjutor and holding by grace and visibly the three-fold office which Christ holds by nature and invisibly, viz.,—the kingly or ruling office, the prophetic or teaching office, and the deific or priestly office.

Scriptural meaning of Peter's name according to ST. AUGUSTIN:

"The Rock which the proud gates of hell prevail not against."—i. e., the Rock endowed with infallibility and indefectibility. (In Ps. contra par. Donati.)

According to ST. MAXIMUS: of Turin (7th Century), Christ shares with Peter not his office alone but His very name and title:

"He to whom the Lord granted the *participation of His own title, the Rock."* (Serm. pro Natal. SS. Petri and Pauli.)

Scriptural meaning of Peter's name according to ST. EPHREM, one of the purest glories of the Oriental Church, the most faithful echo of the Church of Antioch founded by St. Peter himself:

"O my disciple, Simon, I have constituted thee the Foundation of the holy Church and have already named thee the Rock, because thou shalt support my edifice *in its entirety*—[Apostles and all]. Thou art the *Inspector* of those who build up my Church upon earth. If they attempt to build amiss, do thou, O Foundation, repress them. Thou art the Head of the fountain whence flows the stream of my doctrine. Thou art the Head of my disciples." (Serm. 4 in hebd. sancta, n. 1—Hymns and Serm. of S. Ephrem edited by Lamy, Mechlin 1882, vol. 1, p. 412.)

Most eloquently, according to St. Ephrem, does St. Peter's name proclaim both his supremacy and his infallibility.

His supremacy: The authority of the Rock must be commensurate with his responsibility and since he is bound to "support" the Christian "Edifice in its entirety," he must in simple fairness and justice have control over every part thereof. He is, by virtue of his office, the "Inspector" and "Head of the Disciples" and must have power to correct and to "repress." He must, in short, be supreme in authority as well as in responsibility.

His infallibility: "The head of the foundation whence flows Christ's doctrine" must be inerrant. The fountain-head whence flows infallibility itself, truth itself, viz., Christ's doctrine—must surely be infallible, for can an infallible stream flow from a fallible source?

Scriptural meaning of Peter's name according to St. Maximus, Martyr (7th Century):

"As the good Shepherd, Peter received the defense of the Flock, so that he who before had been weak in his own case might become the confirmation to all (the Apostles not excepted), and he who had been shaken by the temptation of the question asked him, might be *a Foundation to the rest by the stability of his Faith....* For, he is called the Rock (a) because he was the first to lay the foundation of the Faith, and (b) because, *as an immovable Stone, he holds together* the frame-work and the mass of *the whole Christian structure.* Peter, therefore, for his devotion is called the Rock, and the Lord is named the Rock by his inherent power, as the Apostle says: 'And they drank of the spiritual Rock that followed them and the Rock was Christ.' *Rightly does he merit to share the name who, likewise, merits to share the work."* (De Petro Ap., hom. 4.)

The holy martyr could not tell us in more forcible language that Peter's name scripturally imports the infallibility and supremacy of its bearer—signifies scripturally one who is "a Foundation to the rest by the stability of his Faith"—one who "holds together the framework and the mass of the whole Christian structure"—one who, in a word, "shares the name and the work" or office of the great invisible Head of the Church.

Again, Peter's name means:

In the estimation of Ignatius of Constantinople (A. D. 869), "Supreme chief; Most Powerful Word."

According to a Roman Council held in 494, it means, "Vicar of Christ."

According to the Council of Chalcedon (A. D. 451), "Sovereign Bishop of Bishops." "Sovereign Priest." "Guardian of the Vine of the Lord."

According to the Bishops of Dardania (A. D. 495), "Apostolic Lord and Father of Fathers."

According to St. Cyprian, writing to Pope Cornelius, martyred in 252: "The Bishop of the most holy Catholic Church."

According to the Eastern Clergy, writing to Pope Hormisdas (A. D. 514): "Chief Pastor and teacher and Physician of souls." "True Pastor and Doctor."

(See Library of St. Francis de Sales: Catholic Controversy, ed. 1886, p. 291—and Ryder's Controversy, 10 ed., pp. 12—20.)

The ancients as well as the moderns, then, saw in the name of Peter a name which caused them to "recognize him as Chief" and as the "infallible confirmer" of the Faith—to borrow the language of St. Francis de Sales. (Cath. Controv., Eng. ed. pp. 239 and 297.)

NOTE V

Peter's name means, scripturally and patristically, the Church's Foundation, Bulwark, Capstone and shining Mark

The divine name of Peter reveals another wonderful prerogative of his, hardly ever adverted to by modern Catholic divines and writers. As we have seen, by the name of Peter Holy Writ designates the office as well as the title of our Lord, the Rock par excellence. Now, Christ was not only the Head of the Church of God: He was, by office, the most shining *mark* thereof. He was both the visible Head and the visible, fundamental, unmistakable mark of the Church. Consequently, the name of Peter signifying, as it does scripturally, the office of Jesus Christ, signifies no less obviously the fundamental mark of the true Church. Where the visible Christ was there also was the Church of God: such was the test-sign of the true Church in the earthly days of our blessed Lord. The same test-sign remains and endures for ever: where Christ's visible "other self" is—where His visible Vicegerent is, there the one true Church is.

The words of the text leave no room for equivocation. "Thou art Rock," says our Lord, "and upon this Rock I will build my Church," not temporarily but for ever, so that "the gates of hell shall not prevail against it:" Matt. 16. 18.

The Church being built on the Rock, it follows that where the Rock is there the Church is. Christ virtually says to Peter: "I myself, the Rock, so long as I remained the visible Rock, i. e., during my whole mortal life, was personally and by office the most shining mark of the Church: so thou also, O Peter, thou the visible Rock, shalt be, as such and by office, my visible continuation as *the fundamental mark* of my Church."

Peter is therefore the highest and most shining mark of the Church—the zenith-mark, the earth-commanding mark that gives conspicuity to the Church. Wherefore does Christ remind us that the Rock on which *His* Church is built is not an underground Rock but "a mountain." Matt. 5. 14.

The Church is not so founded upon THE MOUNTAIN-ROCK as to conceal it from sight. She is built —as our Lord, addressing her as His Spouse, tells us—"in the clifts of the Rock:" Cant. 2. 14.

The Word of God emphasizes three features of the Rock,—viz., its loftiness, its hardness or solidity, and its refreshing honeyed sweetness.

So solid is it (Wisd. 11. 4) that the combined powers of hell and of this world can never break it: Matt. 16. 18.

So lofty is it that it is called "the most highest Rock" (Wisd. 11. 4), and can be seen of the furthermost extremities of the earth, towering above the tide of ages.

According to Holy Writ, "the first" Apostolic Foundation (Peter) "is jasper"— and "the wall" of the Holy City "is jasper," i. e. Peter.

The Rock is therefore both a foundation and a bulwark thrown round about the Church—the foundation rising up all around the Church, encompassing her, spreading itself as a dome over her and terminating in a sign or mark, or pinnacle, as visible to all as the face of the sky.

The Rock is, all in one, the foundation that under-lies—the encircling wall that protects—the cap-stone, the PINNACLE that surmounts, i. e., the divine mark that singles out, or the divine index-finger that infall-ibly points out—the Church of the living God to the continents and to "the isles of the sea." Is. 24. 15.

It is not enough to say, then, that Peter (or the Papacy) "is the first proof of the truth of the Church;" the Word of God goes further and compels us to add that *Peter is the first mark* of the true Church.

CATHOLIC TRADITION inosculates with Holy Writ. For instance, St. Optatus of Milevis (A. D. 370) writes: "In that our chair which is the first endowment, Peter sat first... "This mark"—i. e., the Chair of Peter, *"carries with it* the Angel"—i. e., the one legitimate succession or authority: therefore, outside the Chair of Peter there exists no Church and no succession in the Apostolic line. (De schism. Donat., l. 2, c. 2, and l. 3, c. 9).

St. Maximus Martyr compares the Chair of Peter to "a sun of everlasting light." (Opusc. theol., ed. Combefis, t. 2, p. 72.—See Ryder's Controv., 9th ed., p. 16).

St. Chrysostom calls Peter "the Firmament of the Faith" (On parable of ten talents), "the Firmament of the Church" (In illud: Vidi Dominum, hom. 4, n. 3). So does St. Ambrose (de Virginitate, c. 16). From which it appears that, in the common estimation of the East and of the West, Peter is a mark of the true Church as conspicuous as the sun and the firmament itself. Therefore, according to the same unimpeachable witnesses, the comprehensive term "Peter" designates the most prominent mark of the Church, and is, *in itself*, as profoundly observed by St. Chrysostom, both "the guarantee and the mark" of the infallible Church. (See Wilmers' De Christi Eccl., p. 180).

Enough has been said to prove that, according to the witness of Holy Writ and Tradition, the name of Peter is both the title of our Lord himself and the God-devised one-word-formula converted by the Saviour into a proper name to promulgate to all ages, in one single word, the manifold prerogatives of the visible Head of the Church. No briefer, or more comprehensive formula could be devised—and no better way of popularising the formula could be adopted than the making it, as Christ did, the perpetual name of the greatest historical personage, after Jesus Christ, in the sphere of Church-government.

It is the one term—a term divine in its origin, scriptural in its import, and traditional in its continuity— it is the one term that comprises all the titles of Simon Barjona. If you call him the supreme ruler, or the infallible teacher, or the sovereign pontiff, or the fundamental mark of the Church—you enumerate but one of his titles. But you enumerate them all whenever you name "Peter"; for, you then, ipso facto, name scripturally the successor of Jesus Christ, the visible Head of the Church, her supreme ruler, her infallible teacher, her sovereign pontiff, and her fundamental mark.

We can draw but one CONCLUSION from the evidence already adduced: The name of Simon Peter is unquestionably the scriptural and traditional synonym for "Simon—Christ's successor in office." Consequently, Peter literally affixes to his two Epistles what is now known as the Papal signature. When he compendiously signs himself "Peter," or "Simon-Peter", he thereby scripturally signs himself: Simon the Vicar of Jesus Christ as the visible head and foundation of the Church—Simon the supreme ruler—Simon the infallible teacher—Simon the sovereign pontiff—Simon the first and fundamental mark of the Church—in short, Simon *the Pope.*

Who could exhaust the comprehensiveness of Peter's name? Not all the Councils, not all the Fathers, not all the Doctors of the Church can fathom its supernatural depths. Not only is it a wondrous verbal condensation of all the prerogatives lavished on Peter, but it is *his Divine credential,* for it bears, as a scriptural warranty of the manifold prerogatives it signifies, the royal seal and the sign manual of its Divine inventor, Jesus the Christ.

If we ask: By what right, O Simon, dost thou, a poor fisherman, presume to command the princes of the Church, thy fellow-Apostles and their successors? By what right dost thou rebuke the arrogant prelates "lording it over the clergy" (1 Pet. 5. 3)? Show thy credentials. Where are they? The humble Fisherman instantly replies: "My credentials are in my name. Christ named me and made me what He named me, viz., Peter, the Rock—i. e., Christ's "other self" in office. My name is the Christ-accredited herald of my Vicegerency—the Christ-appointed teacher and preacher thereof—the Christ-issued certificate and proclamation thereof."

Our brief commentary shall not be looked upon as mere rhetoric but as having ample justification in Scripture and tradition, in the eyes of those conversant with patristic literature. Nor need we fall back upon the Western Fathers exclusively for the proof of our assertions. The foremost of the Greek Fathers will again be our favorite authority. Ponder the sublime wonders which St. John Chrysostom finds in the Divine name of Peter. The Saint has already told us that Christ "inserted in Peter's name a *guarantee* and a *mark* of solidity of Faith." If you now ask why Christ attached such a guarantee and sign of infallible Faith to *the very name* of Peter, St. Chrysostom answers: "In order that he"—Peter, *"may use his perpetual name as a special authoritative teacher* of this rock-solidity of his." (In illud: Paulus vocatus etc.— See Wilmers' De Christi Eccl., p. 180).

In other words, Christ's obvious and specific intention, in giving this name and title to Peter, was to enable him to employ it constantly as a God-chosen reminder and mark of the Christ-office vested in its bearer.

The name of Peter is the Christ-given credential, the Christ-signed Letters Patent accrediting Peter to all mankind and to all ages as Christ's successor in office.

Such is the name that Simon Barjona attaches and signs to his Epistles: it is (we repeat) nothing less than *the Papal signature* of the Fisherman: "Simon Peter" and "Simon the Pope," are perfectly interchangeable terms.

What A SHORT AND ROYAL ROAD to the truth as it is in Christ Jesus! Let us repeat with endless thanksgiving: Peter, ever living in his successor, is the Christ-appointed, unmistakable fundamental mark of the one true Church of God.

Now, where is Peter, or his successor? History replies, says the Protestant thinker Leibnitz, at one with Protestant scholarship: The Roman Pontiff alone is the successsor of Peter, the one contemporaneous link in the historic line of succession from Peter to Pius X. He is Peter historically and lineally continued for nineteen centuries. Yet more, Peter, as the fundamental mark of the Church of God, is the more unmistakably identified in his successor in the See of Rome because no bishop on earth but that of Rome ever dared to claim the Petrine succession in the queen city of the universe.

Wherefore the holy Fathers call the See of Rome "the first of the marks of the Church." "Peter therefore," says St. Optatus, "first filled that pre-eminent Chair"—or Bishopric of Rome—"which is the first of the marks of the Church." (De Schism. Donat., l. 2, c. 2, 3, 4).

Notes
(Blank Page In Original)

Second Part

Peter's name proclaims him the
SOURCE
of all Church-power Under Christ

Second Part

Peter's name proclaims him the *source* of all Church-power under Christ.

By Church-power we understand the threefold power vested in the Church by our Divine Lord, viz., the ruling, teaching, and sanctifying power—the royal, prophetic, and deific or priestly power.

NOTE VI

A glance at the names of Jesus and Peter

Over nine hundred times does the New Testament, by means of the very name of Jesus, proclaim the one Saviour of the world. In like manner Holy Writ, by means of the very name of Peter, again and again proclaims the successor of Christ in the office of the Rock—in the headship of the Church. For, in the case of Jesus and Peter above all others, does the name itself express the office they exercise; and, consequently, every mention of the name is a scriptural designation and proclamation of the office attached thereunto.

Holy Writ itself furnishes a full definition of the above names as expressive of a great and unique office. respectively—i. e., Holy Writ teaches us how to regard and use each of the two names referred to not merely as the name of a person but as *God's own definition* of a special office.

The term "Jesus" is therefore a divine definition as well as a divine name—and so is the term "Peter" or "Cephas".

Meaning of the name of Jesus defined by Holy Writ

(a) "Thou shalt call His name Jesus, for He shall save His people from their sins." Matt. 1.21.

Etymologically, "Jesus" means one who saves, a saviour.

Scripturally, it means the Saviour par excellence the one only Saviour from the evil par excellence, viz., sin and its consequences. We say the only Saviour, for Holy Writ affirms that *"He* shall save," i. e., He and no one else, He alone can and shall save.

(b) "This day is born to you a Saviour, who is Christ the Lord:" Luke 2. 10.

Holy Writ defines still further the name of Jesus as signifying the *promised* Saviour, i. e., the Christ or Messiah, nay, "the Lord" who, "born" in the flesh, is literally God Incarnate and manifest in the flesh: 1 Tim. 3. 16.

(c) "John saw Jesus coming to him and he saith: behold the Lamb of God, behold Him who taketh away the sins of the world." John 1. 29.

St. John completes the definition of the adorable Name by telling us *how* He shall take away the sin of the world: namely, by being immolated as "the Lamb of God." "Jesus", then, scripturally means Saviour and victim—Saviour through the effusion of his own blood.

The Evangelist intimates plainly enough that, scripturally, the name of Jesus signifies "the Lamb of God who taketh away the sin of the world;" the Lamb of God, i. e., the Lamb of infinite worth who substitutes His own divine life for our infinite guilt: the true paschal Lamb who, by being eaten, substitutes the life of God in man for the death of sin in man. "Jesus", therefore, means, scripturally, the vivifying Lamb, the *deifying* Lamb as well as the *atoning* Lamb of God.

Does not the Lamb Himself say, in the same Gospel of St. John 6. 58:—"As...I live by the Father, so he that eateth me the same shall live by me." That is, those who receive me worthily are made, not figuratively but really, "partakers of the divine nature:" 2. Pet. I. 4.

Therefore, according to Holy Scripture, the name of Jesus is, truly and strictly speaking, God's own definition of the office of God Incarnate as the Saviour, Vivifier and Deifier of mankind at the cost of the last drop of His blood.

Nor does Holy Writ come to a sudden halt after thus beautifully defining the meaning of the adorable Name. On the contrary, the thrilling import of the divine definition is sunk deeper and deeper into the soul by the scriptural process of iteration. For, inasmuch as the name of Jesus, as defined by Holy Scripture, means God Incarnate redeeming us, deifying us with His precious blood,—it follows that, every time the Name is repeated in the sacred record, the reader is virtually admonished as follows:

"Remember, O man, that God Incarnate has redeemed thee and deified thee with His own blood."

The constant and multiplied iteration of the Name impresses and sinks not only the sound thereof but its divine definition and significance into the heart of the thoughtful reader. Nine hundred and twenty-five iterations of the Name mean nine hundred and twenty-five burning ejaculations from the adorable heart of Jesus.

Nine hundred and twenty-five times therefore does the Word of God cry out: "Remember thou, O reader of the Word: remember thou, O hearer of the Word, that God Incarnate has redeemed thee and deified thee with his own blood."

Viewed in the light of Holy Scripture, the nine hundred and twenty-five iterations of the blessed Name become, as it were, nine hundred and twenty-five celestial aqueducts— the handiwork of the Holy Spirit—spanning the infinite immensities to bring the waters of eternal life, clear through, from the everlasting hills and all the way down to the thirsty deserts of the human soul, converting the barren desolate wastes into ever-singing wells and fountains of life and gratitude and joy.

Or, to make use of another simile—with each repetition of the adorable Name the omnipotent Spirit sings to the responsive soul the old canticle of Israel: "Let the well spring up.... the well.... prepared by the direction of the Lawgiver:" Num. 21. 17. And from the depths of the soul the mystic well springs up in ecstasy divine—up to the very lips of God Incarnate, whose thirst (John 19. 28) it slakes with the sweetly wooing draughts of love.

Such, in miniature,—aye, in infinitesimal miniature only—is the practical result or spiritual fruit of Holy Writ's nine hundred proclamations, *in the one word "Jesus,"* of the saving and self-immolating and deifying office of God's Incarnate love.

Meaning of Peter's name defined by Holy Writ

Because Peter holds the Office of Christ as visible Ruler of the Church, his very *name* holds in Holy Writ a position exactly analogous to that held therein by the name of Jesus. The analogy extends to the same scriptural process of iteration—the iteration or repetition of his office-expressing name: a manifolding process which manifolds well nigh two hundred times the Divine proclamation of Peter's Divine office.

The King's Vicegerent being the official counterpart of his Sovereign, Holy Writ very consistently treats both the person and the name of Peter as the counterpart of the Master in the sphere of Church-government.

We have no less an authority than that of God's written Word to affirm that the name of Peter means that its bearer is, (a) under and with Christ, the alpha or co-beginning of the Church; (b) the visible Rock or perennial source of the entity of the Church; (c) of her authority; (d) of her infallibility; (e) of her indefectibility; (f) of her compactness and solidity; (g) of her one-ness and unicity; (h) of her holiness; (i) of her catholicity; (j) of her apostolicity; (k) the Apostle more deeply beloved of the Lord than any other apostle; (l) the visible Rock or perennial source of anti-pharisaism—i. e. of the restoration of the fallen.

NOTE VII

(a) Peter's name means, scripturally, that Peter is, under and with Christ, the alpha or co-beginning of the Church

"Thou shalt be called Cephas": John 1. 42.   By these words God Incarnate bestows on Simon Barjona three distinct prerogatives—the first of which is enlarged upon by all commentators, whilst the second is frequently overlooked, and the third apparently lost sight of altogether.

The first prerogative sets Peter apart as the successor of Jesus Christ upon earth; the second, as the name-sake of the Lord who delights in calling himself the Rock; the third, as the alpha or co-Beginning, under and with Christ, of the Church universal.

Both in principle and in fact, Christ there and then associates and assimilates Peter to Himself as the first visible Beginning of the Church—as her initial point of existence preceding in time as well as in dignity every other member.   For, Christ was both the beginner and the beginning of His Church—and He here associates Peter to the last-named privilege by using him as the first material, the first "stone" actually laid in the construction of His Church.

(1) Our blessed Saviour sets Peter apart as His successor.   "Thou shalt be called Cephas," i. e., thou shalt be called after me, the Rock; because thou shalt be my successor, and as I am Cephas the First, so shalt thou be, in the order of time, Cephas the Second.

Thou shalt bear my name because, after my death, thou shalt be, in a measure and in the visible order of the Church, that which I will ever remain in the invisible order of the same,—viz., the Rock, the foundation or support, the supreme Head.

"All bow the head by divine right before Peter, and the Primates of the whole world obey him as they do the Lord Jesus Christ Himself," says the Church through the great Eastern Father and Saint, Cyril, patriarch of Alexandria (lib. Thesaur.).

(2) Our Blessed Saviour confers *there and then* on Simon Barjona His own name and title of "the Rock"—"thou shalt be called Cephas"—not in a year or in a month hence—not after my formal appointment of the Apostles only—but henceforward and from this day forth shalt thou be called Cephas. As I personally addressed Abraham, the father of the old Covenant, so do I now address thee Peter, the Father of the New Covenant, and in the same terms: "Thou shalt be called Abraham," said I to Abram of old; "thou shalt be called Cephas," or Peter, do I now say to thee, O Simon Barjona. The words "thou shalt be called Abraham" meant and were understood to mean that Abram was to be called Abraham from that instant, without any postponement or delay. Similarly, the words "thou shalt be called Cephas," or Peter, signify that thou, Simon Barjona, art to be called Cephas, or Peter, from this very moment.

The Church of Spain was deservedly regarded and hailed at the Vatican Council as the queen of scriptural knowledge. Now the current Spanish translation of the New Testament paraphrases John 1. 42 as fol-

lows: "thy name from this very moment shall be,
Rock." (See ad loc. the Spanish translation of Knecht's
Commentary on the N. T.)

In his learned French translation of the Gospel of
St. John, Father T. Calmes designates the first interview of Peter with the Saviour as "the moment of
his vocation." (On. John 1. 42)—

The reader has only to open the Gospel of St.
Matthew (4. 18) to see for himself how clearly the
holy Evangelist intimates that Simon Barjona was already called and known by the name of Cephas, or
Peter, at the time of the miraculous draught of fishes—
i. e., long before the organization of the Apostolic
college (Matt. 10. 1.).

St. Luke intimates the same fact (Luke 5. 8).

Let us revert to the words of the text: "Thou
shalt be called Cephas" (John 1. 42)—i. e., "I do here-
by bestow upon thee, yea, even *now* in presence of thy
brother Andrew (ibid.), my own title of office, as a
pledge of the tremendous office with which I will in
due time invest thee. And the better to emphasize the
importance of thy name, I will once more, in the near
future on a far more solemn occasion, bestow the same
name upon thee before the whole Apostolic college
on the very day of its erection (Luke 6. 14)—to show
that thou art to be the Rock of the Apostles as well
as of the Disciples. Thus did I, in the days of yore,
not once only but on two different occasions, confer
the name of Israel upon my servant Jacob—viz., (a)
when he wrestled victoriously with my angel (Gen.
32. 28), and also when, several years later (b) I ap-
peared to him at Bethel (Gen. 35. 10).

But, as Jacob yields to thee in dignity and in holiness, not twice only but *thrice* will I call thee to the divine ministry in store for thee. Twice shalt thou be called singly and separately (John 1. 42; 5. 10), to indicate thy independent supremacy over and above the eleven other Apostles. And once shalt thou be called jointly with thy brother Andrew (Luke 1. 16), to show forth the necessity of communion with thee in order to be a true Fisherman of Jesus Christ.

Nay, more, in addition to thy triple calling, thrice will I appoint thee the Shepherd, or ruler, of the universal Fold. (John 21. 15—17.)

The Word of God suggests another profound lesson in its treatment of the names of the two Fathers of the two Covenants. Abram's name was changed or converted into another name—Abraham,—even as the true Synagogue was to be converted and merged into the Catholic Church. Simon's name, however, was not *changed* into another, but a *new* name was added to the old one. God Incarnate says not to Simon: Neither shall thy name be called any more Simon" —whilst He did say to the holy patriarch: "neither shall thy name be called any more Abram:" Gen. 17. 5.

The *unchanged* name of "Simon" typifies the changeless, or final, character of the Church of which he is the head; — whilst the *new* name of "Peter" typifies the new splendors of perfection which, under Peter, the *New* Covenant adds to the Old.

But it may further be asked, Why did not our Lord suppress altogether Peter's former name? Because that name was to be a constant, merciful and Providential reminder not alone of Peter's low extraction, but of his sinful past and downfall. And nothing short of such a memento could, humanly speaking, keep Peter's heart and head from turning dizzy with pride—raised as he had been upon the highest, aye, the unutterably sublimest pinnacle of honor and dignity to which mortal man can be raised. For, Abraham's office was but the shadow of Peter's, a mere planet compared with a blazing sun.

"I will remind you," says the profound as well as gentle Doctor of the Church, St. Francis de Sales, "that our Lord did not change St. Peter's name, but only added a new name to his old one—perhaps in order that he might remember in his authority what he had been, what his stock was, and that the majesty of the second name might be tempered by the humility of the first—and that if the name of Peter made us recognize him as Chief, the name of Simon might tell us that he was not *absolute* Chief, but obeying and subaltern chief and head." (St. Francis de Sales' Cath. Controv., Eng. tr. p. 239.)

(3) Both in principle and in fact Christ, there and then (John 1. 42), associates Peter to Himself as the first visible Beginning of the Messianic Church.

"Thou shalt be called Cephas" (ibid), says Jesus to His Disciple. Now, the latter could not justly and properly be called Cephas, i. e., the Rock-foundation, if he lacked the two characteristics of a foundation— and these are (a) *priority of place*, or rank, as the underlying support of the whole structure; and (b) *priority of time,* in the order of construction, over the other parts of the edifice. Therefore, by the very fact that our Lord names Simon "Cephas," i. e., the foundation, He in *principle,* confers upon him priority of time over the rest of the Church. Peter is thereby declared to be the very first material to be used *before* any other in the building of the Church.

Indeed the *name* of Foundation, or Rock, given to Simon implies the *name* as well as the function of "the Beginning"—which is the very name by which our Lord calls Himself in the 25th verse of the 8th chapter of the Gospel according to St. John.

And, in point of *fact,* our Lord does here make Peter "the Beginning," the *earliest* member of the Christian Church.

"Thou shalt be called Cephas"—i. e., "not with the interior voice of my grace only, but with the external voice of my sacred Humanity do I now, at this very instant of time, distinctly and *formally* call thee before any other as my earliest and first disciple. For, the bestowal of my name upon thee is not only a formal calling (Franzelin, Thes. de Eccl. Christi, Romae, A. D. 1887, p. 100)—not only the most emphatic and glorious form of calling—it is moreover the very first *exterior* calling extended by Me to any human being. This honor is neither Andrew's, nor John's, nor Philip's, nor any other's, but thine exclusively, O Peter, as My Word attests unanswerably. "Not only art thou the first of my Apostles by priority of rank —thou art also the first of my formally called disciples by priority of time. I do make thee the initial point and use thee as the initial factor, under and jointly with Me, wherewith to begin the construction of my Church. Thou art the first thus formally called by Me as a Disciple; Philip shall be the second,— Nathanael, the third (John 1. 43)—Andrew, the fourth (Matt. 4. 18)—James and John, the fifth and sixth (Matt. 4. 21)—Matthew, the seventh (Matt. 9. 9) etc.

"'Thy calling antedates the existence of any disciple—it precedes the creation of the Apostolic college (Luke 6. 12), the mission of the Apostles (Matt. 10. 5), and the mission of the Seventy-two (Luke 10. 1).

"John and Andrew visited Me before thou didst, and responded before thee to the invitation of John the Baptist to follow Me (John 1. 37)—but *after* thee only shall they be explicitly, exteriorly and formally called by Me to the discipleship" (Matt. 4. 18, 21).

"Thou shalt be called Cephas (John 1. 42): these words were addressed to Peter even *before* Jesus had called any of His disciples." (McErlane, The Church of Christ the Same Forever, p. 89.)

The distinguished biblical critic, Father Th. Calmes, in his French translation of St. John's Gospel—designates the *first* interview of Peter with the Saviour as "the moment of his vocation." (On John 1. 42.)—

Neither Andrew nor John,—as remarked by St. Augustin—were called at the time of their first interview with Jesus. They were not therefore, as is generally and erroneously believed, the earliest diciples of Jesus. "It is manifest," writes St. Augustin, "that they clave unto Him only *after* He had called them out of the ship." (7th tract on John). The calling of Andrew and John, consequently, did not take place on the occasion of their first visit to Jesus, but later on, when Jesus, says St. Augustin, "called them out of the ship."

Rightly therefore, and for two reasons, does the Evangelist St. Matthew call Peter "the first"—since Peter was the first in rank and the first in time—the first in the hierarchial and the first in the chronological order of the Church of Jesus Christ.

Peter was cast into the official mould of the Christ and is a perfect official cast of the divine Master. Christ in "the form of God" (Philip 2. 6), i. e. as God in Person, is the life-principle of the Church established by Himself. Christ in "the form of.... man" (Philip 2. 7), is the First visible Beginning of the same Church, which is the master-piece of all creation. The sacred humanity of our Lord, viewed in its relations to the Church, is first not only in the sphere of rank and authority—it is also First in the sphere of time, the very first stone, the chiefest corner-stone laid in the construction of the divine edifice (Eph. 2. 20)—Mary and Joseph being, respectively, the virgin Mother and the virgin Foster Father of Jesus and of His Church.

Christ did not begin (as He could) to organize a visible society before He assumed a visible body—v. g. by gathering men together under an invisible head by means of personal revelations made to various individuals. No, He first became Incarnate and was then, as we just said, the first visible Beginning of the

Church—the first in time as well as in power and authority. The more indelibly to impress upon all men the moral necessity of a *visible* head to the Church, He would not allow His Church to begin her existence before His Incarnation.

And, likewise, the more forcibly to teach us that Peter was his "other self" (St. Augustin) in office, his successor in the government of the Church—He made Peter that which He is himself, viz., the First in authority and the First in time or in calling—called before all the other disciples and apostles. Christ *began* His Church—as a society composed of human persons —with Peter, because it is fitting to begin a building with the foundation itself.

Thus do the Disciples rest upon Peter as upon their Beginning and Foundation (John 1. 42); so do the Apostles (Matt. 1. 2; 16. 18);—so do the Jews (Acts 2. 14—41);—so do the Gentiles (Acts 10. 34—48); thus is Peter indeed the vicarious universal foundation of the universal Church. (Matt. 16. 18.)

Our insistence upon this point—Peter's priority in time and in relation to the calling of the disciples—is both warranted and necessitated (first) by its strange absence from the best commentaries on this text (John 1. 42), and (second) by its momentous importance— since it reveals the unsuspected depths of the assimilating process by which Christ assimilates Peter to Himself in His royal, prophetic and sacerdotal office, nay, in His blessed and glorious death on the Cross —as noted by Tertullian and the Fathers generally.

"Oh how happy is this Church," says Tertullian, "where the Apostles poured forth the fulness of doctrine together with their blood—where *Peter was made equal to the Lord* in the manner of his suffering!" (De Praesc. 36. c. 32; Adv. Marc. 4. 5—A. D. 160—240).

Heretofore the one grand feature of resemblance between Christ and Peter ever noticed in this text (John 1. 42) was the promise of the headship to Peter. But, the *other* magnificent feature of resemblance between Christ and Peter shown by the same text, was not even alluded to—i. e. Christ assimilating Peter to Himself by making him, under and with Himself, the incarnate living Beginning of the Church—*the first human personality* used by our Lord in the erection of His Church.

The unfortunate suppression of this last and deep trait of resemblance between the Christ and His Vicar does not do justice to the Word of God, and gives us only one half of the Scriptural portrait of Peter. It shows only one side of the face, viz., Peter's headship in common with Christ, and, leaves out of sight the other side of the profile, viz., Christ imparting to and sharing with Peter His fundamental prerogative as the incarnate visible Beginning of the Messianic Church —Peter being thus made by our Lord the visible alpha and omega, jointly with and under Christ, of the whole Church militant. The alpha: for, the Church *begins* with Christ and Peter in the order of time. The omega: for, the temporal *end* of the Church here below will come with the last breath of the last Pope—when the Church militant will merge forever into the Church triumphant, and time shall be no more. (Apoc. 10. 6.)

NOTE VIII

(b) Peter's name means, scripturally, the visible Rock or perennial source of the entity of the Church

"Thou art Rock and upon this Rock I will build My Church:" i. e., thou art the Rock or perennial source of the visible entity of the Church, since my entire Church is built upon thee; not merely a part or fraction thereof, but my whole Church in her universal entity. Therefore, out of thee, the Rock, there is no Church of Christ, no fragment of it, no particle of it whatsoever.

Jesus Christ pledges His omnipotent word as God Incarnate that He will build His Church upon the Rock, Cephas, or Peter—that, consequently, out of the Rock Cephas, or Peter, Christ's Church is not, does not exist, and that she has no entity whatever except "upon Cephas" the Rock. He adds that, *because* thus resting irrevocably on Cephas the Rock, *His* Church shall triumph for ever: (Matt. 16. 18.)

Ponder the words of Christ. He virtually says: "Without Peter not only can there be no victorious Church, but there can be no Church at all. Without Peter, my Church not only cannot conquer, but she cannot even *be*. Out of Peter no Church of mine shall ever be: no Peter no Church."

The Church therefore owes her very being, as well as her perpetual victory over hell, to the virtue of her Christ-appointed Cephas or Rock—who is thus the permanent instrumental source, not only of her triumph, but of her very being or entity: a truth candidly admitted by unprejudiced Protestants. For instance, Judge Robinson, Professor at Yale College, frankly says: "Uniting with the See of Peter, is to be the Church of Christ. Not to acknowledge the See of Peter, is to form and constitute a *human* organism." In other words, there can be no Church of Christ out of Peter. (An Hour with a Sincere Protestant, by Rev. J. P. M. Scheuter, p. 15, note)—Italics ours.

NOTE IX

"Thou art Rock and upon this Rock I will build my Church, and the gates of hell shall not prevail against it. And I will give to thee the keys of the kingdom of Heaven: and whatsoever thou shalt bind upon earth it shall be bound also in Heaven: and whatsoever thou shalt loose on earth, it shall be loosed also in heaven." (Matt. 16. 18, 19.

That is to say: To thee alone singly and separately and independently, O Cephas, do I promise the keys of my Church, which is the Kingdom of heaven on earth, to show that thy name, so expressive of Christlike authority, is no empty sound—but that all authority shall indeed be instrumentally derived from thee, the Rock: so that whatsoever thou shalt bind or loose by thy own personal and independent authority shall instantly be bound or loosed in heaven. Not so, however, with my other Apostles; under thee alone, and never independently of thee, can they exercise such powers in my Church. Therefore do I not say to any of them as I do to thee "I shall give thee, James—or to thee, John—or to thee, Paul, the keys of the kingdom of heaven." But, after giving thee alone, O Kepha, full and independent authority such as I myself exercise, I will transmit a due portion of the same *from thee* to the other Apostles, not apart from thee but subordinately to thee, the visible Head. (Matt. 18. 18.)

After vesting the plenitude of authority in thee, I will transfuse thereof from thee, the Head, to the Apostolic members united and subordinated to the Apostolic head. As I took out of the first Adam the bodily form of the first Eve (Gen. 2. 21), so, in a manner, will I take out of thee Peter the derivative form of authority to be exercised by thy fellow-Apostles.

This truth is so plainly written on the face of the sacred Record and was so indelibly impressed upon the mind of the Apostolic Church that Tertullian has enshrined it in the following oft-quoted sentence: "If you think the heavens shut, remember that the Lord, here (in Matt. 16. 19), left its keys to Peter, and *through* Peter, to the Church." (De Scorpiace, c. 10.)

The order established by our Lord does not vary with the wind of Error, and the Church ever receives the benefit of the keys through Peter continued in his successors.

The better to impress upon the Church the fact that Peter is the visible source whence flows all authority, Christ begins by investing Peter alone with the plenitude of power in the Church. (Matt. 16. 18; John 21. 15.) In due time the Apostles receive jurisdiction from Christ *and* Peter acting jointly as a moral unit (Matt. 18. 18; Mark 16. 15; John 20. 21)— but they receive it collectively, i. e., corporately;—consequently, they receive it as divinely constituted under their visible head, Peter: for, the head rules the body. In the two orders of nature and of super-nature, guidance (authority) proceeds from the head to the members, not from the members to the head. "Beatus

Petrus et praeferri omnibus Apostolis meruit et claves regni coelorum communicandas caeteris *solus* accepit." (S. Optatus; de Schism. Donat. contra. Parmen., l. 7, c. 3 et l. 2, c. 2.)

NOTE X

Alluding to the invincible strength of the Rock created and established by Himself, our Lord says to Peter: "Simon, Simon, behold satan hath desired to have you that he may sift you"—i. e., all of you, My Apostles—"as wheat, but I have prayed for THEE that thy faith fail not: and thou, being once converted, confirm thy brethren." (Luke 22. 31.)

"I have prayed for THEE that thy faith fail not," that is to say: I have made thee the Rock of Faith, the Rock of infallibilty. For thy fellow-Apostles also have I prayed, asking my Father to bless them as *members* of the Apostolic college—but for thee alone have I asked my Father a special blessing, i. e., that He may bless thee as the visible *head* of the Apostolic body and of my whole Church. As the authority of the Apostolic members is conditioned upon strict union with and subordination to Peter—for nowhere have I given them the power to bind and to loose separately from their head, Simon Peter (Matt. 18. 18)—so is their immunity from error derived from the same source and upon the same conditions. Through Peter alone do I transmit my Keys or authority to the Church, and through Peter alone do I transmit my infallible teaching to her. I might have imparted in-fallibility to every bishop separately and independently.

Why do I not choose to do it? Because I am the infinite Wisdom of God, and human wisdom itself, shortsighted as it is, sees at a glance that a system of independent infallible teachers would open the door to schism and divisions without end. Therefore am I pleased to appoint *one* Apostle alone as the supreme, infallible Rule of Faith, endowing him alone with full independent infallibility—an infallibility which the other Apostles can only share proportionately through the channel of communion with Peter: for, Peter is the Confirmer of *all* the brethren, the Apostles not excepted.

"Satan hath desired to have you" all, my beloved Apostles, "but I have prayed for thee," Peter, "that thy faith fail not."

Here, Christ inferentially says to the other Apostles: Take warning that, if you do not wish your faith to fail, you *must* cling to the center of unity, Peter, for nowhere else but in union with *him* shall you find inerrancy as well as eternal cohesion. Out of Peter there is no Church of *mine*, no Church of Christ, no salvation.

Peter is the centripetal force that keeps the supernatural universe of the Church infinitely more solidly compacted together than any orb in space: for the starry orbs shall one day dissolve and perish, whilst the living Orb of the universal Church shall outlast and outlive all ages and shall endure forever.

Had Christ built his Church upon a *fallible* Apostle or Pope, she would rest on a sand-drift, not on a rock. The Rock guaranteed by our Lord as strong enough to keep the Church secure against the gates of hell

(Matt. 16. 18), i. e., error, is therefore necessarily infallible by virtue of Christ's solemn and explicit guarantee (ibid.)—

Christ makes three distinct assertions, viz., first, that He prayed for the infallibility of Peter's Faith (Luke 22. 32)—second, that His own Prayer as God Incarnate is *always* heard (John 11. 42)—and third, that Peter shall accordingly be the infallible Confirmer of the Faith of his brethren (Luke 22. 32).

Therefore the infallibility of the Church flows from Peter down to the brethren, not from these to Peter: therefore Peter is the perennial visible source of Infallibility.

In Gal. 1. 18, the Holy Ghost uses, in honor of Peter exclusively, a word employed in no other place in the Holy Scriptures: Speaking of St. Paul's visit to Peter, Holy Writ implicitly calls Peter the Divine oracle of the Church. For, the Greek term it employs (istoresai) does not simply mean that Paul called on Peter: it implies that he consulted Peter as a divine oracle. Such is the classical significance of the word in Greek authors—v. g. in Euripides, Ion 1547—etc.— the term being used especially of visits to the oracles of the Deity.

Holy Writ significantly employs quite a different term with reference to St. Paul's visit to St. James. The term used in this instance is "eidon," the common word for "saw." (Gal. 1. 19.)

Scripturally speaking, then, St. Paul saw St. James in Jerusalem, but he *consulted* Peter, there, as the Oracle of the Church of the New Covenent. For, the High Priest of the New Law is not inferior to the

High Priest of the Synagogue—of whom Cruden's Protestant Concordance says: "The High Priest, clothed with the ephod and pectoral, gave a True Answer, *whatever was the manner of his life.*—God had appropriated to his person *the Oracle of His Truth.*" (s. v. Oracle and Priest.)

NOTE XI

(e) Peter's name means, scripturally, the visible Rock or perennial source of the indefectibility of the Church

"Thou art Rock, and upon this Rock I will build my Church, and the gates of hell shall not prevail against it." Matt. 16. 18—i. e., "Thanks to thee, O Peter, who art the Rock of my own creation, the gates of hell shall not prevail against my Church. Neither now, nor in a thousand years, nor in 1600 years, nor in two thousand years, shall they prevail against my Church: *because*, from thee (under me) shall my Church derive a never-failing supply of strength and invincibility. Sect after sect shall pass away, whilst thou alone shalt stand with the Church built upon thee, for thou alone art the Rock built on the rock of my omnipotent Word: heaven and earth shall pass away, but my word shall not pass away." Matt. 24. 35.

Christ proclaims the indefectibility of His Church —i. e., the absolute uninterruptibility of her existence through all ages—(Matt. 16. 18) ; and the reason He assigns for her indefectibility and indestructibility is that she is irrevocably built and resting on Cephas, the Rock, Peter. Therefore Peter is the perennial visible source of the indefectibility of the Church.

NOTE XII

(f) Peter's name means, scripturally, the visible Rock or perennial source of the Church's compactness and solidity

"Confirm thy brethren" (Luke 22. 32)—i. e., *all* thy brethren, all my disciples without exception—Apostles, bishops, priests, clergy, and laity—are to be confirmed, strengthened, consolidated by thee in the Faith and in hope and charity, in closer and closer communion with one another. In thee shall they find immunity not only from the darkness and blindness of heresy but from the sterilising influence of schism.

Thou art the Rock, not for thy sake alone but for the sake of thy brethren. Do not, then, O blessed Rock, keep thy strength unto thyself, but transfuse the strength of the Rock into the universal Brotherhood.

NOTE XIII

(g) Peter's name means, scripturally, the visible Rock or perennial source of the one-ness and unicity of the Church

"Thou art Rock and upon this Rock I will build my Church and the gates of hell shall not prevail against it." "Therefore, by logical impli–cation, the gates of hell *shall* prevail against *all* churches *not* built upon the Rock, Peter. Therefore, moreover, whoever departs from the Rock, Peter, cuts himself off from the very Foundation of *my* Church. For, my Church, in contradistinction to all other churches, is built upon thee, O Rock, O Peter; and there does she abide, not shifting her Foundation from Peter to Photius, or from Peter to Luther or Calvin, or from Peter to any one else,—but remaining forever fixed on the Rock of my choice and creation, Cephas, or Peter.

Therefore, finally, as there is no Church of mine out of the Rock, men must of necessity gather around and cling to the Rock under pain of being left out of my Church. Thus are tribes and tongues and peoples and nations unified in thee and by thee, under Me. And thus art thou, O Rock, O Peter, the wonderful Rock and perennial source of the visible unification of all mankind into one vast brotherhood.

And as thou alone, O Peter, art the Rock of unity, so shall all the churches built outside of thee, be the ever-shifting sands of endless division and confusion. Theirs shall be the burning and blinding divisions and confusions of the stormy sands of the desert when blown about by the simoom.

Thou art by grace, as I am by nature, the Rock against which all the sects or hostile churches shall either grind themselves or be ground to powder: Matt. 21. 44.

The one-ness, or unity, of the Church is the divine prerogative in virtue of which "the Church in all its members and parts forms one entire connected whole" (Klee on the Church—ap. "Catholic" by Monsignor Capel, 1st. ed. p. 26.)

Peter is the Rock of unification: he unifies the members of the Church by the fact that he is the one foundation, the one platform on which Christ requires them all to stand and to cling together.

Christ extols the unifying power of Peter when He appoints him the Confirmer or consolidator of the whole Christian brotherhood (Luke 22. 32.)

For, "Confirmer" means consolidator, strengthener: now strength preverbially lies in unity. Therefore Peter the strengthener means Peter the unifier. Therefore Peter is the permanent instrumental source of the compact one-ness of the Church. He is the living Rock and, as such, communicates to the whole Church the compactness, solidity and unbreakable one-ness of the Rock which he is.

Peter is also the perennial visible source of the unicity, or absolute anti-plurality and absolute indisibility of the Church.

The unicity of the Church is the divine prerogative in virtue of which there cannot be either "a plurality of Christian or co-ordinate churches," or one Christian Church or Kingdom of God divided against itself—as to creed, communion, or authority.

Observe that the one-ness of the Church connotes the *fact* of her unity; the fact that she is one in reality —whilst the unicity of the Church connotes the absolute *impossibility* of there being more than *one* self-same indivisible Church of Christ, indivisible as to creed, communion, and authority.

Besides, whilst the one-ness or unity of the Church is one of her visible marks, her unicity is one of her invisible properties—a property evident to the mind in view of the Word of God, but not visible or perceptible to the bodily senses.

The sense of sight attests the unity of the Church— but reason alone can, under the guidance of Revelation, attest the impossibility, by reason of the express will of Christ, of there being more than one Church of His, and the impossiblity of the Church built on Peter being only a part of, and not the whole Church of Jesus Christ.

(First)—Christ said to Peter: "Thou art Rock, and upon this Rock I will build my Church" (Matt. 16. 18)—not my Churches but My one and only Church. Therefore Christ built one Church only upon Peter, and it is impossible that there would be more than one Church of Christ built on Peter.

(Second)—Christ said to Peter: "On this Rock I will build *My* Church." The Church of Christ being built on the living Rock called in Hebrew *Kepha* (John 1. 42) and in Greek *Petros* (ibid., Greek text)—it follows that, outside of "this Rock" there can be no

Church of Christ—or that it is impossible to make a Church of Christ out of a Church which stands not and is not willing to stand upon "this Rock", Peter.

Now, the two impossibilities just described—i. e., the impossibility of the Church or Kingdom of God being divided against itself as to creed, communion, or authority; and the further impossibility of there being more than one Church or Kingdom of God, i. e., a plurality of co-ordinate Christian Churches—these two impossibilities constitute the unicity of the Church; and Peter is, by divine ordinance, the instrumental source thereof.

As the Christ-appointed Rock of divine strength and might, he is the instrumental source of the Force whence flows the twofold impossibility (1) that the Church built on Peter, and viewed in herself exclusively, should ever be divisible and more than one Church, one vast organism; and (2) that outside the Rock Peter, there could ever spring into being another Church of Christ—because *Peter absorbs all the Church-producing energy available in the Economy of Christ*, and thus strikes with radical impotency any attempt at producing another Church of God.

NOTE XIV

(h) Peter's name means, scripturally, the visible Rock or ministerial source of the holiness of the Church .

Peter is the Rock of the Priesthood, the ministerial source of sanctification, the Church's Stairway to heaven (St. Augustin); for out of the Church of God there is no lawful and acceptable sacrifice; and without the lawful acceptable oblation of the Sacrifice of the New Covenant, there can be no sanctification, but only profanation and sacrilege.

Such is the scriptural meaning of the very name of Peter. Antiquity merely paraphrases Christ's explanation of the name when it says, through St. Jerome, who addresses Pope St. Damasus as the Rock, or Peter: "On that Rock I know the Church is built; whoso eats the Lamb outside this House is profane," i. e., guilty of sacrilege (Ep. to Pope Damasus, A. D. 376).

Mark how forcibly St. Jerome affirms that whoever is outside "that Rock," viz., Peter, and his successors, is by that same, outside the House of God, outside the Church altogether.

Centuries before St. Jerome, the holy prophet David had intimated that the pure honey of sanctification can only be got "out of the Rock."—"And He fed them," says David prophetically, "with the fat of wheat" (His adorable flesh and blood), "and filled

them with honey" (His own Divine Life) "out of the
Rock." That is to say, the God-appointed channel of
the Deific life productive of holiness is none other than
the Rock (Ps. 80. 17).

The prince of the Doctors of the Church, St. Augustin, is even more emphatic than St. Jerome. According
to him, Peter is so essentially and perpetually the foundation of the Church and the ministerial source of her
sanctification as to be her stairway to heaven:

"It was the Lord Himself," writes the saint, "who
called Peter the Foundation of the Church: and there-
fore it is right that the Church should reverence this
Foundation wherever her mighty structure riseth.—
Blessed be God who hath commanded that the Apostle
Peter should be exalted in the congregation! Worthy
to be honored by the Church is *that Foundation
through which lieth the ascent into heaven.*" (15th
Serm. on the Saints: Rom. Brev., Feast of St. Peter's
Chair at Antioch, 22d of Febr.)

NOTE XV

(i) Peter's name means, scripturally, the visible Rock or perennial source of the catholicity or universality of the Church

"The Rock" is the scriptural name of God Himself, and when God Incarnate conferred it upon Simon, He thereby declared that He would put in Peter the strength of God signified by the name: and He kept his promise. Behold the strength of God concealed under the frail form of a frail old man! Behold one single man, a supernatural Samson, not only stronger than all mankind together, but stronger than the myriad-legioned hosts of Satan: Matt. 16. 18.

Peter is the mightiest moral force on earth, the colossal force of a scriptural world-builder. For, the Christ who made him the mighty centripetal or unitive force that compacts the Church into everlasting unity—did also make him the centrifugal or expansive force that expands the unity of the Church into Catholicity, i. e., into a world-wide organism—the living expansive force that enlarges the tiny seed into a world of the first magnitude. (Matt. 14. 31, 32.)

Note that the unity of the Church could exist without her Catholicity. The Church, like the Synagogue, might be one without being universal. But her Catholicity cannot exist without her unity. For, prescinding from the fact that Christ did not promise universality to any other Church but exclusively to the Church

compacted into one visible body under one visible head
called Peter—it is evident that a universal divided body
is a contradiction in terms: for, if divided up into frag-
ments, it is no longer a body at all, much less a universal body. The Catholicity of the Church is not a
universal agreement to disagree, a universal absence
of unity, a universal disruption, a universal Babel, a
world-wide series of divisions and fractions. It is a
universal unit, constitutionally and territorially universal—i. e., a unit constitutionally embracing, at all
times and all over the world, the absolute entirety of
the Church of Jesus Christ—and a unity territorially
extending to the uttermost limits of the earth.

In a word, the Catholicity of the Church *is her own
unity enlarged and universalized:* therefore the producer
and constant enlarger of the unity of the Church is ipso
facto the producer of her Catholicity or universality—
and such is Peter, as we proved when treating of the
unity of the Church.

Contemplating in advance the world-encircling vast-
ness of the Church He was to built on Peter, the
eternal Son of God and future Son of David according
to the flesh, exclaims, prophetically, through the lips
of the royal Prophet: "With Thee is my praise in a
great Church" (Ps. 21. 26)—"I will give thanks to thee
in a great Church." (Ps. 34. 18.)—"I have declared
thy justice in a great Church" (Ps. 39. 10).

So divinely universal is the "great Church"—the
Ecclesia magna—prophesied by David, that her very
enemies cannot help wondering again at her wonderful
Catholicity: "The Catholic idea in religion," says the
Rev. J. L. Jones, a prominent Unitarian preacher of

Chicago, "is today triumphant. The Roman Church has succeeded because it grasped the ideal of Catholicity, of uniformity, of harmony, of oneness. I am not defending that Church as such... Nevertheless, the Roman Church is the greatest social protection ever thrown out of the human heart. It is *the only organization in history that has brought together in any such manner diverse races, hostile nations, and alien peoples.* It represents beautifully our democratic ideals." (Italics ours. See the N. Y. Freeman's Journal, May 4th, 1901.)

"The Catholic Church is the grandest organization in the world," exclaimed a Protestant minister, the Rev. J. G. Thompson, at the morning service held on Sunday, April 5, 1903, at the Independent Church of Christ, Los Angeles, California.

NOTE XVI

(j) Peter's name means, scripturally, the visible Rock or perennial source of the Apostolicity of the Church

I. Apostolicity Defined

The term Apostolicity may be predicated of the original Twelve, of their succession, i. e., the Catholic episcopate, and of the Church herself.

Membership with the Apostolic hierarchy itself constitutes *active* apostolicity.. Simple membership with the apostolic Church constitutes *passive* apostolicity.

1. The Apostolicity of the original Twelve consists in their being the *original* members of the ruling, magisterial and sacerdotal body constitutively headed by Peter, as essentially organized by our Lord in person.

2. The Apostolicity of the Catholic episcopate is the continuity, by means of succession, of the Apostolic Body as organically constituted by our Lord under the one visible head, the one organic centre or bond of unity, of the whole Church: said visible head being at first the visible Humanity of Christ himself; and, after the Passion and resurrection of Christ, Peter—and after Peter, his successors from century to century, down to our own day.

3. Broadly defined, the Apostolicity of the Church is the continuity of the Apostolic Church up to this day—or the continuance up to this day of the Primitive

Church as founded by our Lord and planted by the Apostles.

Specifically defined, the Apostolicity of the Church is the identity of the Catholic Church with the Church of the Apostles.

———————

II. Apostolicity: Its Petrine Source; General View

The striking designations under which Holy Writ mentions Peter and his Apostlic brethren clearly intimate that the Apostles formed a college or body whose head was Simon Peter: For the New Testament frequently designates the Apostles under a collective or corporate appellation as "the Twelve," or, after Judas' suicide, "the eleven"—while it expressly gives to Peter the title of "the First" (Matt. 10. 2).

For mention of the Twelve, see:

Matt. 10. 1, 2; 10. 5; 11. 1; 20. 17; 26. 14, 20, 47.

Mark 3. 14; 4. 10; 6. 7; 9. 34; 10. 32; 11. 11; 14. 20.

Luke 6. 13; 8. 1; 9. 1, 12; 18. 31; 22. 3, 14, 47.

John 6. 68, 71, 72; 20. 24.

Acts 6. 2.

For mention of the Eleven, see:

Matt. 28. 16; Mark 16. 14; Luke 24. 9, 33; Acts 1. 26; 2. 14; 1 Cor. 15. 5.

There be indeed twelve foundations (Apoc. 21. 14) but one single Apostolic bed-rock underlying the eleven other foundations (Matt. 16. 18).

Twelve foundations in the fundamental structure of the Church, but one, and one only, underlies the others; for to one of these only and exclusively has Christ said: "Thou art Rock and upon this Rock"— upon this one bed-Rock—"will I build my Church," my whole Church. Peter, to whom alone these words were addressed, is therefore the one Apostolic bed-Rock upon which the eleven other Apostolic stones rest and abide forever.

There exists, on Apoc. 21. 9—21, no commentary more illuminating and more profoundly beautiful than that of the Anglican divine Paul James Francis, in the 7th chapter of his fine work on The Prince of the Apostles. He says:

"When we examine the twelve foundations in detail, we find that they are of different material. 'The first is jasper; the second, sapphire; the third, a chalcedony; the fourth, an emerald etc.' This shows that God has differentiated the Apostles one from the other in some sort. There is not therefore absolute equality, a distinction of some kind is intended.... Is there no principle of interpretation by which we can discover which of these foundations represents St. Peter? Yes, to be sure we can. We have already noted in a previous chapter that in the four lists given in the New Testament of the names of the Blessed Apostles, St. Peter's name always takes the lead, while St. Matthew expressly calls him the First. The First Foundation then is St. Peter, and we see that it is jasper. But let us give a wider sweep to our vision. We raise our telescope and lo, we make an important discovery. We observe that 'the city lieth four-square. And the building of *the wall of it is jasper.*' Here is something which gives to St. Peter at once an immense distinction. The walls of the Holy City are built out of the material, not of the second foundation, nor of the third, nor of the fourth, nor yet of any of the other foundations, save of the first, and that foundation is jasper as are the walls. Does not this revelation carry with it the whole Petrine contention? Our Lord said to Simon, 'Thou art Peter, and on this rock I will build My Church,' and lo, when we come to view the fiinished structure we find that the walls are built up not of the material of other eleven foundation stones which constitute the Apostolic basis of the Church but of the material of the first, that is to say, of Peter.

The walls of the City do not take their rise from that apostle who is represented by sapphire, nor yet from chalcedony, not from the emerald, the beryl or the amethyst, but only from the jasper. Is not here a distinction which reconciles any seeming conflict of statement between our Lord and St. Paul; the Former saying to St. Peter, 'On this Rock I will build My Church' and the latter declaring that the Church was built 'on the foundation of the Apostles and prophets, Jesus Christ Himself being the chief corner-stone.' "

The Church derives her Apostolic continuity from the Apostolic Body and, by consequence, from the constitutive head, or organic centre constitutive of the same Body. The head is thus the primary visible source of the Church-continuity otherwise called Apostolicity. For, an Apostle is one who belongs to the hierarchial body constitutively headed by Peter, as essentially organised by our Lord (Matt. 16. 18, 19; Luke 22. 32; John 21. 15, 17).

Therefore whoso is not under Peter is no member of the Apostolic body organised by our Lord. But, if one cannot be an Apostle without being a member of the Apostolic body—and if one cannot be a member of the Apostolic body without being under the Apostolic head,under the organic centre established by our Lord as constitutive of the same body—then it follows that Peter is the source of the Apostolicity and continuity of the Apostles themselves, and, consequently, the *capital* source of the Church that derives her continuity from the Apostolic body.

———

COROLLARY—Whoso is outside the foundation, Peter, cannot possibly impart Apostolicity, i. e., Apostolic continuity to the Church, for two reasons: first, because no one can give that which he has not; now, to be out of the Rock, Peter, means to be out of the Christ-established Apostolicity, which is essentially centered in Peter (Matt. 16. 18; Luke 22. 32; John 21. 15, 17). How then can such an *outsider* give to the Church the Christ-established Apostolicity which he himself has not?

Secondly: one who is not even a simple member of the Church cannot possibly be at the same time a *chief* member of hers, i. e., an Apostle or a successor of the Apostles. In other words the Apostolicity of Christ is essentially inseparable from the Church of Christ. One cannot be simultaneously an Apostle, i. e., a chief member, and no member of hers at all. Therefore whoso is out of the Church is ipso facto out of the pale of Apostolicity: whoso is outside the radical membership of the Church is a fortiori outside her *chief* membership, her Apostolic college.

On the other hand we know that—Christ having built His Church on the one visible foundation, Peter —whoso is outside of the Rock, Peter, is ipso facto outside the Church of Christ, out of which there can be no Apostolicity: therefore whoever is outside the Rock, Peter, is outside the Christ-appointed sphere of Apostolicity.

III. Apostolicity: Its Petrine Source—a Closer View

Four elements constitute Apostolicity of rank and office, viz., (first) membership with the Apostolic hierarchial body essentially headed by Peter, as organized by our Lord in person;—(second) the power to rule the Church of God;—(third) the magisterial power to teach;—(fourth) the sacerdotal power to offer the clean Oblation and sanctify the members of the mystic body of Christ the Catholic Church.

Now, we have shown that Peter is the visible source of Apostolic membership and of the threefold power just named: therefore Peter is the visible source of the Apostolicity of the Church.

Note: the ruling, teaching, and sanctifying powers may be regarded as the active matter of Apostolicity —whilst the sovereign headship of Peter is the essential *form* or condition of Apostolicity.

Schismatic and heretical bishops and priests are utterly destitute of Apostolicity, since they lack its four constitutive elements.

(a) They lack the first element, viz., membership with the Apostolic body or college essentially headed by Peter at command of the Lord himself. Peter is the Christ constituted head of the Apostolic body (Matt. 16. 18; Luke 22. 32; John 21. 17). Now, members severed from the head no longer possess *corporeity,* and likewise apostles or bishops severed from the Apostolic head, Peter, lose, by that same, Apostolic corporeity or Apostolicity. For Apostolicity, or Apostolic corporeity, is where the Christ-appointed head thereof is, not where the amputated member lies.

A Peterless Apostolicity is a headless Apostolicity, and a headless Apostolicity is not Christ's Apostolicity, and therefore no Apostolicity at all.

With still greater cogency does this argument apply to the heretics and schismatics' utter lack, not only of Apostolic membership, but of Church membership altogether. For we know that, the better to perpetuate and strengthen the unity of his Church, Christ ordained that outside the Rock, Peter, there can be no Church of God whatever (Matt. 16. 18). Therefore heretics and schismatics, being outside the Rock, Peter, are ipso facto outside the Church of Christ altogether. Not being even simple members of the Church, how (we ask again) can they be at the same time her chiefest members, i. e. her Apostles or rulers?

Such a contradiction would be a piece of infinite folly infinitely beneath Infinite Wisdom Incarnate.

(b) Heretics and schismatics lack the second element of Apostolicity, viz., infallibility in teaching Faith and morals.

A bishop, or any one else, cut off from the Apostolic head, Peter, is by that very fact cut off from the infallible magisterial power which, by the express will of Christ (Luke 22. 32, etc.), is to be derived from him alone for whom alone Christ's prayer asked and obtained infallibility (ibid.)—and whom alone Christ, accordingly, established Confirmer of the Faith of His brethren throughout the whole Church.

Therefore bishops who secede from Peter forfeit the Divine promise of Confirmation in the Faith (i. e. infallibility) made to Peter. They repudiate the divinely established Confirmer of the Faith (Luke 22.

32), and become thereby, scripturally speaking,—they and their deluded followers—"the blind leading the blind." (Matt. 15. 14.)

We Catholics have, then, the warranty of Scripture, besides the Catholic experience of nineteen centuries, to back us when we affirm that those cut off from Peter *cannot* preserve the true Faith; much less can they teach it infallibly, as they themselves explicitly acknowledge, since they never tire of repudiating all claim to magisterial infallibility.

In the first place, they deny, by the very fact of their schism or separation, the cardinal doctrine of Jesus Christ—the unity of the Church. For, Christ affirms that *His* Church cannot exist out of the Rock, Peter, upon whom He built it—whilst *they* affirm that Christ's Church can and does exist outside its Christ-appointed foundation, Cephas or Peter. (Matt. 16. 18.)

Apart from this radical departure from the palpable teaching of Jesus Christ, they invariably fall into other grievous errors: v. g. the Eastern schismatic body errs grievously touching the procession of the Holy Ghost. Some of them—for instance, the schismatic patriarch of Constantinople—err even about the valid form of baptism, falsely teaching that the immersed alone are validly baptized—a gross error, so palpably unscriptural and unhistorical that even the schismatic Church of Russia refuses to countenance it.

Let us suppose, however, the existence of a phenomenon never witnessed heretofore, viz., the actual preservation of the true doctrine of Jesus Christ *outside* the society which He founded for the avowed

purpose of preserving His teaching in its purity and
integrity—a phenomenon which would disprove the
necessity of the Church established by our Lord in
order to perpetuate and propagate His doctrine. Let
us grant for a moment that such or such a person,
though outside the Church, has actually preserved the
identical faith or doctrine taught by our Lord; it would
by no means follow that such a phenomenal mortal is
a member of the Apostolic hierarchy, or even of the
Apostolic Church itself. His pure faith could not give
him active Apostolicity, i. e., could not make him a
member of the Apostolic hierarchy—since all the true
Disciples of our Lord had the true faith and yet *only
twelve of them* were raised the Apostolic office. Nor
would the pure faith of such a unique individual give
him even passive Apostolicity, i. e., make him a member
of the Apostolic Church—since many secret believers
in the Gospel of Jesus Christ were nevertheless too
cowardly to join His Church and lived and died out of
it—and since, moreover, many a believer—for instance,
Simon Magus—was cut off from the pale of the
Church notwithstanding their public adhesion to the
true Faith.

It stands therefore scripturally and logically established that integrity of doctrine suffices not to confer
either active or passive Apostolicity, i. e., membership
either with the Apostolic hierarchy itself or with the
Apostolic Church.

(c) Heretics and schismatics lack the third element
of Apostolicity, viz., the power to rule the Church of
God.

To Peter alone did Christ commit the Key of sovereign authority (Matt. 16. 18; Luke 22. 32; John 21. 15,

17)—and consequently a bishop disowned by Peter, so far from having power to rule the Church of God, does not even belong to the one Fold essentially joined to Peter as the body to the head or the house to its foundation. Not only has such a bishop no power to rule, but he has no authority nor commission to preach or to administer the sacraments.

(d) Heretics and schismatics lack the fourth element of Apostolicity, viz., the restoring, sanctifying, deifying, power of the priesthood.

To Peter alone did Christ commit in sovereign trust the *lawful* use of the Sacerdotal Key of sanctification (ibid.), whose Divine source is the lawful oblation of the unbloody Sacrifice of the New Law.

A Christian cut off from the Church still preserves the indelible character of his baptism. Likewise, a bishop cut off from the See of Peter still preserves the indelible character of the ordination and the sacrificial and sacramental power inherent in his sacerdotal character. But he loses the sanctifying power of his priesthood. That is to say, his offering of the sacrifice is neither lawful nor acceptable to God. For, as under the old law, the Temple's altar was the only one on which the one lawful and acceptable sacrifice could be offered to Jehovah—so, under the new Law, Peter is the one Christ-chosen Rock and Altar-Stone, whereon the true Sacrifice may be lawfully and acceptably offered to God:

Whoso offers or eats the Lamb outside the Rock, Peter, offers and eats outside the Divine foundation of the Church—i. e. outside the Church herself; and

such an one, to quote St. Jerome once more, "is profane"—i. e. abhorrent to God. (Letter to Pope St.
Damasus.)

A dilemma:

The schismatic Oriental bodies and their off-
shoots have never been able to face the following de-
lemma:

Either the old, primitive Peter-headed Church under whose headship they were from the very first and
remained for several centuries—is Apostolic, or it is
not. If it is not Apostolic,then the seceding branches
could derive no apostolicity from the parent-trunk and
cannot be apostolic. But if the Church whence they
seceded is Apostolic, as they acknowledge it is—then
the seceders therefrom have seceded and been excom-
municated and amputated from the Apostolic mother-
Church, the Church of the Rock, against which, says
Christ, the gates of hell shall not prevail (Matt. 16.
18).

In either case, they lack Apostolicity or Apostolic
corporeity.

NOTE XVII

(k) Peter's name means, scripturally, the Apostle more deeply beloved of the Lord than any other Apostle

A very important distinction should be insisted upon here— a distinction overlooked by the moderns but sharply drawn by the Fathers—between the love of tenderness (as, for instance, that of a mother for her new-born babe) and the love called "of intensity or preference," as, for instance, the love of the same mother for her first-born and full-grown son. The first was vouchsafed by our Lord to St. John alone, and the second to Peter exclusively among the Apostles.

The fact that Peter was the Apostle most deeply beloved of Jesus is clearly established not only by the testimony of the Fathers but by the clear witness of the Lord himself. Christ in person answers affirmatively the question to which Peter, in his profoundly touching humility, would not return an affirmative reply, viz., "Simon, son of John, dost thou love me more than these?" For, straightway after questioning Peter thrice, Jesus says, "Feed my sheep." As if to say: "Because I know that thou lovest me more than these other Apostles of mine, therefore do I in return love thee more than I do these; and I accordingly intrust thee, in preference to them, with my treasure, my Spouse, my Church."

As noted by the Fathers, especially the deepest of them all, St. Augustin—St. John loved Jesus more *tenderly,* but Peter loved Him more *intensely,* more ardently. And, in return, Jesus loved John with a more tender, but Peter with a stronger and intenser love. "Thus parents love their little children with a tender love, but those who are youths or grown up with a stronger and more solid love: whence also they give greater gifts to them than to the little ones." (Cornelius à Lapide on John 2. 17: Mossman's translation.)

St. Chrysostom shares the convictions of St. Augustine and exclaims: "Rejoice, O Peter, thou who didst love the Lord with a burning soul, thou the *most* faithful of *all* the Apostles." (Rom Brev., Oct. SS. Peter and Paul)—It were blasphemy to contend that "the most faithful," i. e. the most God-loving "of all the Apostles" was not, by a just recompense, the best beloved of God—since our love of God can only be the immediate effect of God's love for ourselves and, consequently, the most authentic evidence thereof.

Tertullian, born a little over half a century after the death of the Apostle St. John, gives voice to the tradition of the Apostolic Church—then so fresh and vivid among Christians and even among heretics—that Peter was, without exception, "the best beloved of the disciples: carissimo discipulorum." (Adv. Marcion. 4. 13.)

St. Optatus tells us that Peter "deserved to be preferred to *all* the other Apostles: beatus Petrus et praeferri omnibus Apostolis meruit" (De schism. Donat. contra Parmen. l. 7. c. 3. et l. 2. c. 2). That is to say: Peter's greater love for Christ justly entitled him to the greater love shown him by our Lord.

It is objected that our Lord intrusted His blessed virgin Mother to St. John and not to St. Peter. The reply is obvious. Our Lord did intrust His ever bles· sed Virgin Mother to St. John; but He intrusted *both* the Blessed Virgin and St. John himself and all the other Apostles and all the disciples and the whole Church universal to Peter, and not to John.

Another objection is, that St. John recognized the Saviour from afar on the shore (John 21. 4 to 7) because of his virginal character.

Answer: The *fundamental* revelation of Christianity, viz., the Godhead of Christ, was revealed by the Father in person to the *married* Peter, not to the virgin John. St. John re-echoes St. Peter in the sublime first chapter of his Gospel. John is the eaglet whilst Peter is the parent-eagle whose wings lift up John to the heights of the Godhead, teaching him to face the Son of the living God and the Sun of righteousness.

Even the Jacobites of the far East recognize the significance of the unique trust reposed in Peter. Bar-Cephas, metropolitan of the Jacobites of Mossul (A. D. 890), in the 7th chapter of the second treatise of his book on the Priesthood, pointedly observes:

"Christ Himself did not confer" the High-Priesthood "upon the virgin John, full of zeal though he was besides, but on the *married* Simon, who had also experienced weakness by denying Him." These words are quoted approvingly, and as part of the tradition of the Syriac Church of Antioch, by the Catholic Syriac archbishop of Mossul, Cyril Behman Benni, in his book on the tradition of the Syriac Church of Antioch p. 45.

Christ therefore loved "the married Simon," more deeply than "the virgin John," and gave Simon a "greater gift," viz., the care of His universal Church. (See Corn. à Lap. on John 21. 15—17.)

———

NOTE XVIII

(1) Peter's name means, scripturally, the Rock or perennial Source of anti-pharisaism, i. e. of the restoration of the fallen—the uplifter of the down-trodden and of the fallen

Caution:

We charitably remind the ubiquitous Pharisee who denounces, and affects to regard, the restoration of the sinner as a "license to sin," that he calumniates God Incarnate and His Church—that God is the Father of the *repentant* prodigal, not the father of the impenitent sinner—and that the Divine plea of Christ, of Peter and of the Church, is exclusively in favor of the repentant.

Neither God nor His Church can take favorable cognisance of the wilfully incurable. Nor does God, or His Church, restore those guilty of such crimes against human society as necessitate, for the preservation of the same, the absolute excision, or at least the temporary "binding," of its dangerous membeirs, v. g., murderers and moral degenerates.

Pharisaism, so pitiless to the returned prodigal and so slavishly subservient to Dives and to the shams who serve Mammon in the name of Religion—Pharisaism alone, (not the Church) extends the right hand of fellowship to certain classes of underhand criminals, unhung and unjailed, whose state of impunity and freedom constitutes not only a danger and a menace to society, but a cancer eating up its vitals and its very core.

I. A glance at the Scriptural and Patristic view of Peter as the restorer of tde fallen

"And thou, when thou art converted, confirm thy brethren.... Feed my sheep." (Luke 22. 32; John 21. 15—17.)

The words of our Lord contain a promise, a lesson and a command: the promise of a prerogative, a lesson of humility and humanity, and a stringent command to practice the two last-named virtues—and, consequently, to treat Peter's full restoration as a precedent to be imitated by the ministers of Jesus Christ in dealing with repentant sinners.

The prerogative includes the unsequenchable light of infallibility which crowns the Rock-beacon of the Church, and the inexhaustible force of consolidation and restoration ever flowing out of the same Rock.

The lesson of humility and humanity is conveyed with the infinite delicacy of the adorable Heart, in His loving allusion to fallen Peter: "And thou, when thou art converted," which carries with itself the pledge of a *full* pardon. Yes, "when thou art converted"—for thou thyself shall need conversion, O Peter; and because thou hast boastfully exalted thyself above all thy brethren (Mark 14. 29), thou shalt fall beneath all of them. Thou alone wilt deny me thrice (Luke 22. 34); thou alone wilt deny me with an oath (Mark 14. 71); thou alone among Apostles wilt be a perjurer (ibid.) and a thrice confessed renegade: (Luke 22. 34.) Nevertheless, I will raise thee up and fully restore thee.

The command which follows is positive and sternly unconditional: "confirm thy brethren." That is to say: Treat them all as I have treated thee. Confirm the strong, strengthen the weak, restore the erring and the fallen. Extend to the fallen the treatment which thou, the fallen bishop and apostle, didst receive from Me. Crush not the bruised reed and quench not the smoking flax (Matt. 18. 20), but receive and restore them both.

Restore thy repentant brethren, be they simple communicants, or priests, or bishops.

Do not merely lift them up and forthwith leave them *unrestored* in the way—poor, helpless and life-long cripples to be trampled upon as the living daily footpaths of the pious pharisee and as the living public . highways of pharisaism at large. Restore them in full, even as I did restore thee in full, requiring of thee no other test than the public profession of thy repentant love and amendment: (John 21. 15——17.)

"And thou, when thou art converted, confirm thy brethren."

And lest it be pharisaically believed that the priest or bishop who denies my Church—even as thou, O Peter, didst deny, not my Church alone, but my own Self personally—is forever beyond the hope of restoration, behold, I restore thee as a standing Divine refutation of such a pharisaic doctrine. For, the lesser the dignity the lesser the guilt, and therefore the fallen priest or bishop is certainly not the peer in guilt of the fallen Apostle and Pope-elect. Thus the higher the office the deeper the downfall, and therefore the lapse of a simple member of the priesthood cannot be accounted equal in depth and heinousness to the lapse of his superior.

Nor can thy prompt repentance—just a few hours after denying thy God and Saviour—change the *nature* of thy crime and alter its original enormity which loses none of its intrinsic awfulness. The magnitude of a particular sin is not measured by the length of time spent in its consummation, but by the depths of the ingratitude and treachery which it reveals. Satan's very first sinful thought of rebellion, after one single instant of duration, sufficed to insure his eternal doom. And Judas' infamous sale of God-Incarnate to His murderers, though effected in a few brief moments, shall ever remain the blackest stain on the face of time.

What a fall was thine, O Peter, when thou didst intimate to my murderers that, so far from believing in my doctrine, or in my Church, or even in My-self, thou didst not even *know* Me! Thy denial of Me was a public repudiation, not of my Church alone, not of my teachings alone, but of my very Person. It was virtually an act of radical and supreme apostasy; though, in thy secret heart, thou couldst not help clinging to the Faith.

———

"And thou, when thou art converted, confirm thy brethren."

The greater the grace received the less excusable the recreant recipient thereof. Now, not one of the erring sheep of the priestly Order shall ever be bless-ed as superlatively as thou hast been, O Peter. For thou hast been blessed (a) with the bestowal of my own Divine headship over the Church, even before my ascension to heaven; (b) with the boon of my visible Presence and companionship for three years; (c) with the revelation of my divinity, directly vouchsafed thee by my heavenly Father and at my prayer; (d) with the sight of my miracles, many of which were wrought for thine own especial benefit. Thou hast seen me heal the sick and raise the dead. Thou hast been the eye-witness of the instantaneous raising of Lazarus from the putrefaction of the grave to perfect health. In a word, thou hast known Me and even seen Me at work for three years as the sovereign Lord of life and death.

But, remember, not one of my poor lapsed priests and bishops will, in the future, enjoy such extraordinary blessings and safeguards against a possible denial of the divinity of my Church.

Be thou then, O Peter, both their uplifter and their restorer; the more readily because, though thine own remorseful conscience (not I) upbraids thee as a thrice-renegade priest, a thrice-renegade bishop, a thrice-renegade Apostle, a monster of ingratitude and cowardice sinning with eyes wide open against the known Incarnate Truth—yet do I restore thee fully and unconditionally. I inflict upon thee no banishment to the deserts of Egypt, to live there in perpetual seclusion—no deposition from thy episcopal rank and office—no removal or transfer to some obscure remote mission or diocese: no, but *solely* because of thy public repentance and conversion (John 21. 15—17), I proclaim thee clean and free from the stain of the past and heroically worthy of the highest and most conspicuous office in My Church.

Wherefore, O Peter, thou likewise shalt pardon and restore thy repentant fallen brethren of the priesthood and of the episcopate. Heed my Father's command: Leave not the anointed prodigal waiting at thy door in the rags of misery and ignominy. "Bring forth *quickly* the first robe" and put it on him (Luke 15. 22). Hear the divine command, O Peter: "Bring forth quickly the first robe," that is to say, that very same robe "which he was wont to wear before he left his Father's house" (Corn. á Lapid. ad. loc). Bring forth quickly, aye, quickly the robe of sacerdotal dignity he wore before, the robe of restoration—not the convict's garb, not the robe of disgrace woven by Pharisaic hands—but the robe of restoration with which I clothed thee, O Peter. Put it on the prodigal —and bring it forth "quickly," since deferred hope maketh the heart sick.

Let the reparation be as public as the offence— and let the restoration be as public as the reparation through repentance.

Let the good and edifying example of the penitent be as public as the scandal.

Let the lips that have publicly taught error still more publicly proclaim and preach Catholic truth.

Let the light and life of the penitent shine far and wide, and hide it not under the bushel: (Matt. 5. 15.) Not thine own history alone, O Peter, but the history of the Prodigal as well, cries out with the voice of God that the repentant sinner must be pardoned and *restored.* A pardon without restoration is a pardon with the gallows. Study the inspired account of the Prodigal's return: for, "all these things—the ring, the shoes and the fatted calf—show the delight of the Father, i. e. the joy of God and of His angels at the conversion of a sinner, and teach that, by the great mercy of God, a penitent is restored to the *same,* or even a *better* position than that which he held before he fell into sin." (Corn. à Lap. on Luke 15. 23.)

Heed not pharisaic scandal-takers, even as I heed them not and am not deterred by their constant clamor of 'scandal, scandal,' from pardoning and restoring thee, O Peter. Join me, thy Saviour, in saying to them, "Depart from me" (Matt. 25. 41) and from my Church, O ye scandal-takers who esteem yourselves too good to remain in a Communion whose visible head is the repentant fallen bishop Simon Peter. And know ye that, for all time to come and for your eternal confusion, there shall be no Church of Christ and no salvation out of the Church and communion of the once fallen priest, bishop and Apostle, Peter. Out of the Church and communion of the restored renegade Peter, there is nothing in store for you, O Pharisees, but everlasting damnation."

The full restoration of Peter is not an exception, not a transient freak of mercy worthy of admiration only: it is a precedent, a Divine precedent, a standing precedent set up by the Saviour in the face of all ages to *command* and enjoin its faithful observance, whenever possible, upon the successors of Peter and of the other Apostles.

II. A beautiful lesson—a sublime injunction faithfully obeyed by the successors of Peter

(First)—Christ sets up the fully restored Peter as *God's own monumental protest against Pharisaism* in the Church and particularly in the sanctuary. To that end, He commands Peter ever boldly to stand up as the Christ-appointed, living antidote against Pharisaism, whose satanic object is to antagonize and nullify the pardon and restoration of repentant sinners: for Satan has sworn eternal enmity and eternal warfare against the fallen race of man. God Incarnate and clothed with our nature arouses the unfathomable envy and hatred of the fallen Angel.

Lest it should be taught (or even thought) that the fallen bishop or priest is forever debarred from full restoration, Christ Himself restores Peter, the fallen high-priest and commands him to do likewise to others: "confirm thy brethren," is the order and command reminding Peter that the blessing of full restoration is not the exclusive privilege of the prelacy or of the laity.

(Second)—To show that the spontaneous maker of a public profession of repentance and amendment is —before God and Angels and men worthy of the Christian name—*no longer* a fallen priest and bishop, but *a true hero* deserving of the highest honor and to be regarded and *treated* as such in His Church— Christ personally crowns a repentant fallen priest, Peter, with the crown of sovereignty over His divine kingdom.

(Third)—Yet more, in order to give the finishing blow to Pharisaism, our Lord decrees that all His official representatives, even to the consummation of ages, shall receive their powers exclusively—aye, that the entire Church herself shall receive the benefit of applied redemption exclusively—through the hands of the thrice-renegade-priest-bishop-apostle Simon Peter, the one divinely appointed connecting link between the hierarchy and the Church, and between the Church and her Founder.

The vicars of Jesus Christ, from Peter down to Pius X, in their Christlike practice of the restoration of the lapsed, both of the clergy and of the laity—have strictly obeyed the Master's injunction, some of them even at the cost of terrible persecutions, nay, of a cruel death brought upon them by the fratricidal machinations of clerical pharisees.

And the one *essential* test required by the Holy See for priestly or episcopal restoration, was the one test required by our Lord of Peter, viz., a public profession of repentant love and amendment, duly recognized by the visible head of the Church. (John 21. 15—17.)

Note carefully that the canonical penance inaugurated in the third century only, and eventually abolished altogether, was nothing (as judiciously remarked by the Jesuit Father Castelein in his treatise on "Rigorism") but a temporary "system of moral police adapted to these rude ages", and consequently could form no *essential* part of either sacramental or ecclesiastical restoration, since it was not required either by our Lord in the case of Peter or subsequently by His vicars in many other historical cases—for instance, in the notorious case of the Donatist priests and bishops who had apostatised from Catholic unity.

St. Augustin rightly says that the discipline of the Church was set aside in their favor. Not. that the Church ever ceased to regard Peter's *public* profession of repentance as adequate to secure absolution from apostasy itself and a fortiori from schism; but because, in this instance, the Church mercifully refrained from requiring even such a *public* profession from Donatist bishops and priests—and because, moreover, these were guilty not only of schism but of heinous anti-social crimes, v. g. mutilation, murder, and other revolting outrages against Catholics. Now all the Church asked them, as schismatics and criminals besides, was, in sign of repentance, to embrace the true Faith and submit to Peter. The moment they did submit, they were allowed to retain their rank and office ; a course eloquently applauded by the great St. Augustin as being in every way worthy of the successor of Peter, the vicar of Jesus Christ.—The Petrine test alone was required by Leo XIII of several priests who had lapsed into the old Catholic Schism, notably the renegade bishop Kupelian (A. D.) 1879), who, after deserting the Catholic Church, had sacriligiously received episcopal consecration at the hands of schismatic bishops and placed himself, as Patriarch, at the head of a schismatic faction among Catholic Armenians.

He was restored in full by the Holy Father after a spiritual retreat of *a few days* in a convent near Rome.

III. St. Augustin's restoration and promotion.

But far more significant than Bishop Kupelian's is the restoration, coupled with the most exalted promotion, of Augustin, the son of Monica, or rather the son of her tears.

We shall condense into a few lines the history of Augustin as told by himself in his immortal Confessions. We give the reference to book and chapter to enable the reader to verify the correctness of our statements.

Augustin, according to his own account, was:

(1) *An apostate*: when 19 years of age, he apostatized from the Catholic Faith of his earliest infancy: Conf. l. 4, c. 1; l. c. 11, etc.

(2) *Nine years a Manichee*, i. e. a notorious renegade far worse than a Christian turned Mohammedan, for Manicheism was far more degrading than Mohamedanism: Conf.   4. c. 1—.

(3) *A rabid propagator of Manicheism* for several years: Conf. l. 4. c.   l. 6. c. 7.

(4) *For years a public calumniator of the Church and a mocker of her sacraments* : Conf. l. 6, c. 3, 4; l. 5, c. 9.

(5) *Twelve years a notorious renegade* or public denier of God Incarnate, viz., from the 19th to the 31st year of his life: Conf. l. 7, c. 19.

(6) *For sixteen years the notorious "slave of lust,"* as he calls himself: Conf. l. 6, c. 15.—viz., from his 16th to his 32d year: Conf. l. 2, c. 3; l. 8, c. 5.

(7) *For sixteen years an obstinate rebel to the grace of God* and to the tears and example of a great

heroine, his own blessed mother St. Monica, who for so many years was a slow-martyr to maternal love and duty.

Such was Augustin when he returned to the Catholic Faith. No sooner had the Church ascertained the sincerity of his repentance than she folded him to her maternal bosom. She not only restored him, but promoted him (first) to the priesthood and (second) to the episcopacy. She crowned him with honor as the soul of her Councils (4th Council of Carthage) and as the wisest counselor of the Vicar of Jesus Christ.

The Church followed the example of the heavenly Father in his treatment of the Prodigal, and the example of Christ in His treatment of Peter. She acted, as the Father of the Prodigal and Christ Himself did, on the principle, (we repeat), that the reparation should be as public as the offense—that the good example of the convert should be as notorious as the scandal given—that the lips which publicly taught error should still more publicly proclaim and preach Catholic truth—that the life and light of the penitent should not be throttled and extinguished under the bushel, but should shine far and wide "to *all* that are in the house," of God: (Matt. 5. 15, etc.)

Indeed St. Augustin assures us that our Lord Himself, as well as His Church, would not suffer the converted sinner to bury himself in solitude, but urged him to devote his life to the holy ministry, as the best way to repair the scandalous past. In other words, Christ and the Church and natural equity and reason unite to cry out that a public offense naturally calls for a public reparation.

This explains why the Church made Augustin preside over a Council in the very city of Carthage, which he had formerly scandalized by his misdeeds.

Was the Church wrong? Did not Christ in person promote the repentant renegade High Priest of the New Law, Peter, to the promised office at the head of the Apostolic college and of the very Church he had so grievously scandalized?

Nay, more, even under the old Convenant of Fear, did not Jehovah *promote* to the High Priesthood, after the first sign of repentance, the recreant High Priest-elect of the old Law, Aaron, and set him over the very nation he had so basely scandalized by openly sanctioning its apostasy and idolatrous worship of the golden calf?

Who but an out-and-out Pharisee will hold that the restored priest or bishop authorized to minister before God Incarnate present on our allars—should be deemed unworthy to minister before the people? Is the people purer than God Incarnate? Such populolatry is but another base form of idolatry, and goes hand in hand with the degrading worship of Mammon so rampant in this country.

IV. St. Augustin persecuted by taunting Pharisees.

The greatest Doctor of the Church, St. Augustin, had for a life-time to suffer the persecutions of taunting pharisees. Ah those taunting pharisees, do they not suggestively put one in mind of the street-dogs that heed no public notice to commit no nuisance, and respect not even public monuments. Hence it is that that monumental pillar of the Church, Augustin, did not escape the nameless humiliation and affront. Indeed, the immaculate whiteness of the monument and its heaven-reaching loftiness were but additional incentives to pharisaic defilers.

In his third sermon on the 36th Psalm, the Saint replies as follows to his pharisaic taunters.

"Thou revilest my past ills: what great things dost thou therein? I am severer against my ills than thou: what thou revilest I have condemned. Would thou wouldst imitate me, and thy error also become past! Those are past ills, which they know of especially in this city (Carthage). For here we lived ill, which I confess.... Yes, *whatsoever I have been, in the name of Christ it is passed."* (Footnote, page 223 of Conf. St. Augustine, Revised from a former translation, by Dr. Pusey, London, 1887.)

Note, en passant, that the Church allowed, nay urged Augustin to preach, *as a bishop,* to the very people who had *witnessed* his former scandalous life. "Those are past ills," he says in his sermon, "which they know of especially in this city: for *here* we lived ill, which I confess."

He was obliged to preach a sermon "lest his character be stained." (Ibidem, page 225, note—)

It is plain that there were those, in the days of Augustin, who "would fain have undervalued his defences of the Faith on account of his sins" (ibid. p. 223). They ostracised or boycotted him and his books. They stenched his name and his writings; a process servilely copied by our modern pharisees.

.The cowardly assailants of the great Doctor were not, however, as a rule, of the household of the Faith, and could not therefore compare in depth of moral cowardice and perfidy with our own pharisees, who can boast the superior and privileged dishonor of being traitors in the very camp of the Church militant.

Little did the mighty moral and intellectual Titan imagine that the 20th century would see—not heretics indeed—but some of his own self-styled spiritual children, indirectly cast up the past to him by imitating his pharisaic persecutors. And, among those self-styled children, not Martin the Apostate but certain diminutive orthodox little Martinettis, noble by birth perhaps but ignoble by character assuredly,—for, alas, they are not ashamed to unearth and rake up the dung of pharisaic taunts, once thrown up into the face of their assumed spiritual Father,—in order to fling it anew in the eyes of priests long since restored by the Holy See.

With what indignation would the grand imperial soul of Augustine disown such bastard natures and declare them in no way connected with his genuine spiritual progeny!

———

V. The challenge of Christ and of His Church to Pharisaism

Could our Lord more forcibly impress upon mankind that the fundamental function of His Church is to restore the fallen—than by making a repentant *public* sinner the living foundation of His Church?

We repeat the question in a more direct form: Could our Lord more forcibly impress upon mankind that the fundamental function of His Church is to restore the fallen—even fallen priests—than by making a repentant renegade priest, Peter, the living Foundation of His Church?

Aye, we *must* put the question in a still more pointed form:

Could our Lord more forcibly impress upon mankind that the fundamental function of His Church is to restore the fallen—even fallen bishops—than by making a repentant renegade bishop, Peter, the living Foundation of His Church?

Day and night and at morn and at noon and at eventide, does the multitudinous voice of the Church upon whose dominion the Sun of God never sets, shout and clamor louder than a million thunders:

Hear ye, O Pharisees, Christ made a repentant *public sinner* the living Foundation of His Church.

Hear ye, O Pharisees, Christ made a repentant renegade *priest* the living Foundation of His Church.

Hear ye, O Pharisees, Christ made a repentant renegade *bishop* the living Foundation of His Church—the head-fountain whence the ministry of salvation must forever flow to the rest of the human race.

Every Catholic bishop is episcopally descended from the repentant renegade bishop Simon Peter......

"God allowed" Peter "to fall, because He meant to make him ruler over the whole world, that, *remembering his own fall*, he might forgive those who should slip in the future." (S. Chrys. Hom. 73 in Joan. 5: ap. Chapman's The Catholic Claims, chap. 5).

Thus is the restoration of Peter, Christ's eternal challenge to the Pharisaism which depraves the heart and satanises the soul of man.

Thus is the restoration as well as the promotion of Augustin, of bishop Kupelian, and of so many others, the everlasting challenge of the Church to Pharisaism and all its foul satanic brood; yea, foul and satanic, for God Incarnate Himself tells us that Pharisaism is the foul offspring of Satan: John 8. 44; Matt. 23. 27.

**The Church honors the penitent priest or bishop as a true hero.
She looks upon his persecutor, the taunting Pharisee,
as a human insect torturing a moral giant**

The Church teaches through the Vicar of Jesus Christ that the bishop or priest who *spontaneously* confesses his sin and retracts his error—not to get thereby a morsel of bread, but on the contrary, at the cost of great sacrifices—is verily a martyr to duty and performs an act of exalted heroism in the estimation of heaven and of all men worthy of the Christian name.

"Indeed," said Leo XIII to such a penitent, "indeed, to humbly acknowledge one's fault, to confess it, to detest it *publicly* and to make amende honorable for it, is *assuredly the most difficult of virtues;* and this, according to the infallible judgment of divine Wisdom, instead of humbling and degrading, ennobles and elevates the soul of him who has been able to achieve such a victory. In the face of such brilliant example, *all remembrance of past faults is wiped out,*" and consequently, the repentant bishop or priest "by this act gains," not full restoration alone, but "glory before God and man."

Such was the Allocution addressed by Leo XIII, on the 18th day of April in the year of grace 1879, to bishop Kupelian who, as we have said, had apostatised and sacrilegiously received episcopal consecration from schismatic bishops.

Why does the Church honor the restored priest as a true hero and lifelong martyr to duty?

Because, unless prepared to buy his way back into social recognition by bribing his persecutors—for Mammon covers a multitude of sins in pharisaic circles, and the pharisee is quite a cheap piece of merchandise—the restored priest must make up his mind either to sink into despair or to practice daily acts of heroism and suffer a lingering martyrdom as long as he lives. For alas "oppression troubleth the wise and shall destroy the strength of his heart:" Eccl. 7. 8.

His perseverance, under such daily provocations to despair and such daily invitations to suicide, can only be secured by a miracle of the grace of God. And therefore the fact alone of his perseverance makes him worthy of being revered above others, as a heroic brother—a myriad-martyred brother.

For, apart from his public confession and heroic recantation which, according to Leo XIII, prove in their author the exercise of "the most difficult of virtues,"—apart also, sometimes, from the sacrifice of brilliant positions of a life of luxury which he could have easily secured, or even retained, by remaining out of the Church,—he must stand twenty, thirty, forty years of slow death at the hands of the pharisee-host.

He must be the daily prey of the clerical blackmailer, of the pious blackmailer, of the worldly blackmailer —the worst of whom is the first, whilst the second is a human emetic.

He must swim across life's ocean with the millstone of the pharisee-world hanging around his neck.

He must wade for a life-time through a sea of

bitterness so deep that all existing pharisees, even if superposed upon one another, could not tower above it but would quickly disappear under its raging billows.

He must cleave his way to heaven through a harder barrier than flint, through an army of pharisees who bar the passage. He must prove stronger than that army: he must be, morally, a ten-thousand-man power in one single person.

And alas, and alas, and forever alas, he must be, as long as he lives, no longer a Diocesan priest but a Diocesan cuspidor..... For, the restored priest, deemed good enough for the Bishop of bishops in Rome, is not good enough for the Pharisee!

But "the soul of the wounded hath cried out, and God does not suffer it to pass unrevenged" (Job 24. 12).

His daily prayer therefore is the sad Scriptural invocation: "I beg, O Lord, that thou loose me from the bond of this reproach, or else take me away from the earth." Tob. 3. 15.

O Pharisee, what art thou but a poor miserable human insect before the superhuman stature of thy restored brother? Bow down before him and humbly say to him in the words of Holy Writ: "thou art worth ten thousand of us": 2 Kings 18. 3.

The pharisee is odious to our Lord because he is not simply a renegade: he is a double renegade, for when he denies that the Prodigal is his brother he thereby denies that the Father of the Prodigal is his own Father. The eternal Justice of God has thus ruled that they who deny the Prodigal deny the Father of the Prodigal and bear the stigma of double-dyed traitors and renegades.

"Despise not a man that turneth away from sin, nor reproach him therewith: *remember that we are all worthy of reproach*" (Ecclus. 8. 6).

O Pharisee, ever prating about "fallen priests", remember that even a fallen dog is better than a standing dunghill—which every pharisee is. And remember also that certain creatures can never fall, for the simple reason that there exists nothing lower than their own natural level.

O taunting pharisee, remember there is something incomparably viler than the very dung of the past; and that nameless something is the born scavenger-soul that delights in the dung, unearths it, feasts upon it, and dwells and abides in it as its native microbe. The very dogs loathe to unearth one another's dung: rise up to the level of decent animal instinct.

Whenever you crown yourself with the disgrace of your fallen brother, you crown yourself with a crown of dung, and you confess yourself beneath the refuse of the past since you use it as your crown and you put your brow *beneath that* crown: the brow is lower than the crown that surmounts it!

To fall is human; but to trample upon the fallen is monstrous—monstrous cowardice and satanic.

O taunting pharisees, impostors and fratricides alike, who *tearfully* preach the parable of the prodigal whilst stealthily and slowly murdering your own restored brother. In vain has your restored brother shed a baptism of tears and wept a baptism of blood: Neither tears nor blood can move the soul of the pharisee. And now, behold, the blood of your brother slowly butchered to make a clerical holiday.... yes, the blood of your brother....

is upon your hands, and upon your head and upon your soul. That fraternal blood cries vengeance to heaven and will haunt the judgment seat of God. Vengeance is mine, I will repay, saith the Lord (Rom. 12. 19).

O blessed Peter, uplifter of the downtrodden and restorer of the fallen, protect thy poor helpless priests from those "lording it over the clergy:" 1 Pet. 5. 3.— for those lords "are shut up in their own fat and their mouth speaketh proudly." (Ps. 16. 10.)—

"It is enough; now, O Lord, take away my life... It is better for me to die than to live... for many dogs have encompassed me." (Tob. 3. 6; 3 Kings 19. 4; Ps. 21. 17.)

Who but a Pharisee will doom to the life-long degradation of a life-long quarantine a fully restored brother holding a clean bill of health from Peter's own successor in person!

Newman's Rebuke to our Pharisees.

"It is our *duty* to love repentant sinners *just as if they had not sinned.*"—We must not "treat them in any degree (God forbid!) *as if their approach were a pollution*" to us.—"If Christ condescends to be their meat and drink, *surely the holiest of men need not scruple to wash their feet.*"

(Newman: Saintliness not forfeited by Penitents, in Sermons on Subjects of the Day.)

NOTE XIX

Comparative view of the threefold power vested in the Church

I. The power of Jurisdiction and the power of Order.

(a) Their general nature:

The power of Order gives sacramental power over the real body of Christ for the salvation and sanctification of souls.

The power of Jurisdiction gives authority over the mystical body of Christ, i. e., power to rule the members and subjects of the Church.

The power of Order is purely ministerial or instrumental—i. e. it can only transmit, but cannot either produce or fashion, that which constitutes its object, viz., the real Body and the grace of the sacraments of Jesus Christ. God alone creates grace and He communicates the same through the ministry of His living instruments—the episcopate and the priesthood. Priests and bishops are only the channels, the dispensers—not the creators or producers or fashioners—but the mere Dispensers of the Mysteries of God: 1. Cor. 4. 1 ; John 1. 33.

The power of Jurisdiction is not instrumental or ministerial, but sovereign. It not merely transmits but produces and makes the laws and precepts which constitute its object: Acts 15. 28, 29, 41 ; 20. 28 etc.

In short, the power of Order is the mere transmitter of its object, viz., the real Body and the grace of Jesus Christ—whilst the power of Jurisdiction is either the producer or the fashioner and framer of its object, viz., its own orders, commands, precepts, legislation and ruling control over the mystic body of Christ, the Catholic Church.

Chief scriptural references: Matt. 18. 17; 28. 20; Luke 10. 16; John 10. 2—5; Acts 14, 22; 15, 16, 29, 41; 20. 28; 1 Cor. 5. 3—5; 7. 6, 10, 12; 11. 2, 34; 2 Cor. 13. 10; Eph. 4. 11; 1 Tim. 1. 19; 3. 2; 4. 14; 5. 19, 22; 2 Tim. 1. 6; 2. 17, 18; Tit. 1. 5; 1 Pet. 5. 2, 4, etc.

(b) Their respective hierarchy:

Three degrees of the power of Order are of Divine institution, viz., the episcopacy, the priesthood and the diaconate.

Three degrees of the power of Jurisdiction are of Divine institution, viz., the papacy, the episcopacy and the priesthood.

(c) Their genesis and form, or frame:

Both are of God. But whilst the power of Jurisdiction comes directly from the visible head of the Church—the power of Order springs directly and immediately from Christ in the sacrament of the same name.

The first (jurisdiction) is mediately of God and immediately of His Vicar; the second (order) is indirectly or instrumentally of the Church and immediately of God who alone can *create* in the soul the indelible character of His Divine priesthood and the Deific gift of divine Order.

The power of jurisdiction is not, so to say, ready-made or specifically determined in advance by the will of God. It is broadly outlined, not mapped out, by our blessed Lord: Matt. 18. 18, etc. Its outlines are to be filled out by Peter or His successor, the pope, who is the Christ-appointed disposer, and grantor of the power (Matt. 16. 18. 19.) in such proportions as he sees fit.

The power of Order is, so to speak, ready-made, i. e. specifically determined in advance by the will and ordinance of Christ—as to its matter, form, subject, minister, and scope. God Himself, not the Church, is its framer and immediate grantor in the sacrament of which the bishop is the ministerial instrument only.

In brief, Peter has dominion and authority over the power of jurisdiction: he may abridge or recall it, or divide and subdivide its field, as he deems best for the welfare of the Church.

But he has no such dominion or discretionary authority over the power of Order, which he can only use in its divinely set form and fixed measure: he is not the disposer and granter thereof, but its mere instrument of transmission.

(d) Their mode of transmission:

The power of jurisdiction is transmitted by appointment or delegation.

The power of Order cannot be delegated, but can only be transmitted sacramentally, through the sacrament of ordination.

(e) Their separability:

The power of jurisdiction may exist without the power of Order, and vice versa. The first may be delegated by the proper authority to one who is not in sacred Orders, to a simple cleric or even to a layman—whilst the power of Order may be conferred on one from whom jurisdiction is withheld partly or altogether.

There is but one sacrament the validity of which depends on the union of the two powers of Order and Jurisdiction viz., the sacred tribunal of Penance, which is essentially judicial in its very nature. Now, judgment can only be passed on one legally subject or amenable to the juage, i. e. upon one over whom the judge holds legal jurisdiction. Impossible, therefore, to render judgment in the sacrament of Penance without adequate jurisdiction over the penitent.

(f) Their respective irrevocable or revocable character:

The power of Order in the Church is as irrevocable as the character imprinted by the sacrament: for instance, a priest or a bishop can never lose the power of consecrating validly the matter of the Sacrifice of the New Law.

But the power of Jurisdiction is revocable at the discretion of the Vicar of Jesus Christ: Matt. 16. 18, 19.

(g) Their respective apportionment:

The power of Order can only be conferred in equal and immutable measure on each priest and bishop: it is fixed, abiding, unchangeable.

The power of Jurisdiction is conferred in varying and unequal measure upon clerics of the very same degree of Order, according to the needs of the Church. Nay, it may vary, be increased or diminished in the same individual and though the latter remains in the same rank of Orders. For instance, a priest, whilst remaining simply a priest, may be promoted in the jurisdictional scale and exercise quasi-episcopal jurisdiction as administrator of a diocese—or may be granted a far greater amount of jurisdiction than any bishop, v. g. as Papal legate.

(h) Their immediate effect:

The immediate effect of the power of Order—besides the sacerdotal character it imprints—is the sanctification of the Church ex opere operato. It produces the world-wide cohesive force of *a world-wide unity of divine life and love* throughout the universal Church.

The immediate effect of the power of Jurisdiction is to produce the world-wide cohesive force of *a world-wide unity of action* throughout the universal Church: its ultimate effect is our sanctification ex opere operantis.

The main points of difference between Order and Jurisdiction are thus admirably recapitulated by Monsignor Capel:

"It will be remarked that in appointing these pastors there was (1) 'imposition of hands' and (2) 'being sent.' (Heb. 13. 7, 17; Acts ch. 13 and 6. 6....) The 'imposition of hands' is the sacrament of Orders, and, in common with the other sacraments, its effect is conferred direct by God.... But the 'Commission' or 'being sent' is derived direct from the Apostles. It specifies where, how, and when the divine authority is to be exercised by the individual pastor... These two powers are distinguished as the power of Order and the power of Jurisdiction. Both are of God: the one comes direct through the sacrament of Order; the other indirectly from God through the Church by appointment.

In the early Church they were often conferred
simultaneously: still they were looked upon as distinct
operations. The power of jurisdiction is not necessarily attached to Orders; though for some acts, such
as absolution from sin, both are necessary. The Apostles and the Seventy, who were sent out at first two
and two, had jurisdiction but not Orders. A man may
be a bishop and yet not be a bishop of a diocese. On
the other hand, a duly and canonically confirmed
bishop-elect possesses jurisdiction without the episcopal
power to confirm and to ordain. A deposed bishop
is still possessed of his episcopal power, but he is
deprived of jurisdiction or cure of souls. His ordina-
tions would be valid; his absolutions null and void.

The power of Order gives capacity; the power
of jurisdiction permits the use of authority. The
distinction between 'can' and 'may,' the former ex-
pressing *inherent*, the latter *dependent* power—affords
a good illustration of the subject. The dispenser of the
power of Order is but an instrument, the grantor of
the power of jurisdiction exercises authority and dominion. The first, coming directly from Christ, is abiding, unchangeable, and is conferred in equal measure
on each priest or bishop. The second, not coming
immediately but through the Church from Christ to
individuals, is conferred in varying proportions as
may be deemed expedient for the good of souls."
("Catholic," 1st ed., p. 23.)

II. The power of Jurisdiction and the magisterial or teaching power

(a) Their respective extent:

The jurisdiction of the Church extends to her own members and subjects only.

Her magisterial infallible prerogative embraces all mankind.

(b) Their respective functions:

The magisterial power is the infallible eye that descries the truths of Revelation. Its function is to make known, expound and define the Divine law and doctrine.

The jurisdictional power is the right arm of the Church. Its function is to enforce, defend, and vindicate her magisterial decisions by means of laws, precepts, and penalties.

(c) The different character of the obligation they generate:

(First) The magisterial power demands of all, per se, the obedience of divine faith due to God the Revealer.

The Jurisdictional power demands, of its subjects only, the obedience of ecclesiastical faith in the precepts of the Church.

The first requires the adoring obedience due to God alone; the second, the reverent obedience due to God's representative, the Catholic Church.

In the ex-cathedra pronouncements of the magisterial power, the motive of obedience held out by the Church is that God himself was in the past the direct and immediate Revealer of the truth of which she is the simple promulgator—and that, by consequence, a denial or non-acceptance of these truths is a direct and immediate disobedience, nay a giving the lie, to God the Revealer in person.

On the other hand, the Church tells us that God is not the direct author or revealer of her own ecclesiastical laws—which consequently cannot command the adoring abedience we owe to the word of the Revealer. A violation of the laws of the Church connotes direct disobedience to the enactor of those laws, viz., the Church herself—but constitutes simply an act of indirect disobedience to God who founded the Church indeed, but is not, after all, the immediate framer of her own laws, precepts, and ordinances.

(Second) When the Church, in her magisterial capacity, promulgates a truth as part of the deposit of Revelation, the consequent obligation of divine faith and adoring obedience is, per se, universal and as irrevocable, as immutable, as the truth she promulgates. But when the Church, in her ruling, or governing capacity, enacts a law or issues a command—the consequent obligation of absolute obedience is *not* universal and is, moreover, revocable and mutable at her own wise discretion. It is not universal, since it goes no further than the law itself which cannot bind the unbaptized and which frequently concerns only a portion of the Church—v. g. the clergy, or the religious orders, or the laity. It is revocable at will, and not immutable, since the Church is free to abrogate, suspend, or modify her own laws.

(*d*) The immediate framers of their respective object-matter:

God is the direct author of revelation, which forms the object-matter of the magisterial power.

The Church herself is the direct author of ecclesiastical law, which forms the object-matter of the jurisdictional power.

(e) Their immediate effects:

The immediate effect of the magisterial power is to produce the world-wide cohesive force of *a world-wide unity of faith* throughout the universal Church.

The immediate effect of the jurisdictional power (as mentioned above) is to produce the world-wide cohesive force of a world-wide unity of action throughout the universal Church. (Cf. Franzelin's posthum. thesis on the Church.)

NOTE XX

Did all the Apostles receive their jurisdiction from Christ exclusively?

Peter alone did. The other Apostles received jurisdiction both from its creator, Jesus Christ, and from its original Apostolic possessor (Peter) as from a visible joint-source of authority. That is to say, both Christ and Peter—the first, by His own independent sovereign will and with the full knowledge of the other apostles (Luke 24. 42, etc); the second, by his own responsive and concurrent will—both Christ and Peter caused the plenitude of authority till *then* locked up in the Apostolic head (Matt. 16. 18, 19; John 21. 15—17), to fill up the entire Apostolic body: Matt. 18. 18.

Even as the Father imparted His authority to Christ (John 20. 21, etc.), and then jointly with Christ (John 21. 15, 17) imparted the same to Peter but in subordination to Christ—so did the latter first impart it to the other Apostles, but in subordination to Peter: Matt. 28. 18.

The profoundly significant fact that authority was first infused into the Apostolic head *alone,* and thence subsequently diffused into the whole body, most forcibly intimates that such a diffusion of authority was brought about by the will of Christ and the *concurrent* will of its Apostolic possessor. For, of a certainty, when our Lord made Peter, under and with

Him, the foundation and visible head of the Church (Matt. 16. 18; John 21. 17), and at the same time deposited in him alone and separately the fulness of Apostolic authority (ibid.)—He thereby declared him the material or *passive* source, at least, of said authority—since the head is naturally the source whence the body derives light, guidance, and governance.

Now, God did not leave His grand work unfinished and half done: therefore does He, in Matt. 18. 18, distinctly forewarn the Apostles that the *then* material source-elect of authority (Peter) must be prepared to become, later on, the *active and formal* source thereof. How? By filling up the whole body therewith, by a positive act of His own will, under the express will of Christ, as recorded in Matt. 28. 18.

Nay, more, the very promise of Christ to all His Apostles, in Matt. 18. 18. that the authority first deposited in Peter (Matt. 16. 18; John 21. 17) would eventually be transfered to the rest of the body— was tantamount to a twofold notice served long in advance upon Peter and upon his fellow-apostles. To Peter it clearly signified: "Be prepared, O thou my chosen Apostolic head, to co-operate with Me by a *positive* act of thy will in the distribution of authority from the Apostolic head and actual possessor thereof, thyself, to the other Apostolic members."

To the Apostles it obviously meant: "Be prepared, O ye my Apostles, to receive authority, now wholly resident in Peter, from the concordant will of Peter and Mine own."

Our Lord does not make, in Matt. 18. 18, the absurd promise that the Apostolic members shall share the inalienable headship of Peter—for, then, their body would only be a many-headed, a twelve-headed monstrosity. What Christ does promise to the Apostles *collectively* taken, i. e. to the whole Apostolic body *as constituted by Himself under the headship of Peter,* (Matt. 16. 19; John 21. 17 ,etc.) is this: Full authority shall naturally descend from the head to the rest of the body (Matt. 18. 18), but always (bear in mind) under the supremacy of the Christ-appointed head, Peter: Matt. 16. 18; John 21. 17.

Thus the Apostles will derive their authority from Christ and Peter jointly, and will exercise it as faithful members, and consequently in perfect subordination to the Apostolic head appointed by our Lord. (ibid.)

The profound truth to be insisted upon is that the above-mentioned circulation of authority from the Apostolic head to 'the Apostolic members will be brought about by the will of Christ and the obediently concurrent will of the Apostolic head, wherein the aforesaid authority was first deposited and permanently resides.

The rash assertion that the other eleven Apostles, besides Peter, received jurisdiction from Christ *exclusively* and not from Peter simultaneously, would, if true, create the reasonable presumption that the successors of the Apostles, the bishops, do still receive it in the same way, i. e. as the pope does, immediately from our Lord and *from no one else.* The proposition, as it stands, is but a half-truth and fatally mischievous as well as misleading. The whole truth is that eleven of the Apostles received jurisdiction

from Christ and Peter jointly and simultaneously—
Peter alone remaining the one *visible* source of authority after the ascension of our Lord.

Such is the teaching of the Holy Fathers: For instance, St. Optatus writes without hesitating that the
other Apostles received the Keys from Peter: "Beatus
Petrus et praeferri omnibus Apostolis meruit et claves
regni coelorum *communicandas caeteris solus accepit.*"
(De schism. Donat. centra Parmen., l. 7, c. 3. et l. 2,
c. 2.)

Pope St. Leo the Great is as emphatic as St. Optatus, and says: "If Christ willed that the other rulers
should enjoy aught together with him" (Peter) "yet
never did He gave save *through him* what He denied
not to others." (Serm. 4.)

It was meet, in fine, that the Apostles should receive juris
diction from Christ in person, the better to remind us
all that Christ is the meritorious efficient *cause*, not
less than the original source, of authority in the Church.

It was equally meet that the subordinate eleven
Apostles should receive jurisdiction from Peter jointly
with Christ—to remind the Apostles themselves that
Christ's Vicar was then, yes, even *then*, the visible
source of Apostolic authority.

It was meet, in fine, that, after His ascension, Christ
should safeguard the prestige and strengthen the hands
of His Vicar by leaving the latter behind Him as the
one visible source of jurisdiction in the Church
militant.

NOTE XXI

Comparative powers of Peter and of the other Apostles

As to the power of Order, the other Apostles were the peers of Peter.

As regards the power of jurisdiction and the magisterial power, they were his subordinates.

(a) Peter received his authority, as we have seen, from Christ exclusively.

The other Apostles received theirs both from Christ and Peter jointly and simultaneously.

(b) The authority of the other apostles was limited to the Christians *outside* the Apostolic college itself, over which they had no jurisdiction.

Peter's authority alone extended over the Apostles, over each of them individually and all of them collectively, and over the whole Church. He could give precepts and commands to the Apostles, dispense from their laws, repeal these and replace them by laws of his own.

(c) The authority of the apostles was conditioned on their adhesion and subordination to Peter.

The authority of Peter was unconditional and supreme.

(d) The other apostles were bound, under pain of schism, to affiliate all the Christian communities they established, with the person of Peter: else, they had failed to build on the visible foundation laid by the Lord, viz., the Rock, Peter.

Peter was under no such obligation toward his fellow-Apostles: they must build on the Rock, not the Rock on them.

(e) The personal infallibility with which each of the other Apostles was endowed was a temporary and exceptional privilege intended to meet temporary and exceptional exigencies,—and, above all, was conditioned on their adhesion to the Rock-confirmer of the Faith: Luke 22. 32.

Peter's infallibility belonged to his office as the Confirmer of the Faith (ibid.), and must needs be as permanent as the Petrine or Papal office itself. Note that whilst, on the one hand, the subordinate jurisdiction of the Apostles and their individual infallibility were conditioned on their adhesion to the Vicar of Jesus Christ,—they had, on the other hand, been confirmed in grace and received a Divine promise of perseverance in their loyalty to Peter. Such is the teaching of Divine Tradition.

(f) Peter alone—singly, separately, independently —received a unique and universal commission from the Founder of the Church: Matt. 16. 18, 19; Luke 22. 31, 32; John 21. 15, 16, 17.

The other Apostles received collectively and corporately, i. e. as already constituted by our Lord under Peter—a general and collective commission only: Matt. 18. 18; Mark 16. 15; John 20. 21.

Their individual jurisdiction was thus plainly declared by the Lord Himself to be, firstly, subordinate to their visible head, Peter; and, secondly, restricted or limited—since it was not the plenitude or universality, but a mere component part, of their corporate authority under Peter. For, a power divided among several is necessarily bounded, in each participator, by the boundaries of undue interference with, or encroachment upon, one another.

It is quite otherwise with powers conferred separately upon one single individual. Here, for instance, is a fact of colossal magnitude and significance: all the powers conferred on the Apostles corporately (Matt. 18. 18; 28. 18); had been previously conferred on Peter singly and individually (Matt. 16. 18, 19; John 21. 17). But the converse does not hold, since the four great prerogatives granted to Peter were never extended to the other Apostles: Peter alone was the Rock (Matt. 16. 18; John 1. 42), the Keyward (Matt. 16. 19), the Confirmer of the Faithful (Luke 22. 32), the universal Shepherd. (John 21. 17.)

The words of Christ, "Go ye into the world" (Mark 16. 15) were addressed to all the Apostles collectively and corporately under their God-appointed head, Peter; they did not and could not apply to each of them individually. Excepting the universal Shepherd's, every Apostle's sphere of action was necessarily restricted by that of every other brother Apostle. In point of fact, tradition, history, and ancient liturgies of the East and of the West attest that—before their final dispersion—the Apostles districted out and apportioned the world among themselves under the headship of him whom Christ had set over them as the universal Pastor (John 21. 17). Each therefore of the other Apostles had a portion of the earth allotted to his share— but Peter had previously received from Christ in person the whole world as his diocese or field of operation: John 21. 17.

Neither Holy Writ nor tradition breathes one word in favor of the untenable opinion that every Apostle enjoyed universal jurisdiction: an opinion which cannot stand the test of deep thought and thorough research. To elucidate:

The jurisdiction of Peter was universal, ordinary, i. e. inherent in his office.

The jurisdiction of the other Apostles was limited and twofold. It was ordinary and extraordinary, or delegated. Their ordinary jurisdiction did not extend beyond the special field allotted to each when, before parting and taking leave of one another, they (as we have said) divided the world into districts under and by the authority of the visible head, Peter—as attested by St. Leo the Great, in his first sermon on SS. Peter and Paul. (Rom. Brev., 18th of January.)

Their extraordinary jurisdiction extended beyond their allotted sphere, but only so far and as often as required by the good of Religion. Now, the interest of religion did certainly not require that the jurisdiction of every one of the twelve Apostles should comprise all the clergy and all the faithful diffused over the face of the globe. In other words, the interest of religion did not require the existence of twelve Peters, but of one and one only, to wit: the one Peter named after Himself, by our divine Saviour: the one universal Shepherd, the one visible center and the one visible bond of unity. It was enough that each of the other Apostles should have, not universal dominion, but a limited though extraordinary jurisdiction extending as far as circumstances demanded, and no farther.

We repeat, one Rock was enough, and God did not create twelve Peters: infinite Wisdom indulges not in superfluous creations. To illustrate: St. Paul's ordinary jurisdiction covered the immense regions evangelised by himself. Beyond that line, he possessed delegated jurisdiction only, in places evangelised by the other Apostles and subsequently visited by himself— v. g. in the Church of Rome, founded by Peter. But his jurisdiction, either ordinary or delegated, was not universal. It did not reach, for instance, the province of the Apostle Thomas in India, nor that of the Apostle Simon the Cananean in Persia etc.

As already stated, the good of souls called not for a Church-wide extension of authority in every Apostle, but for an occasional extension, limited by the requirements of arising emergencies.

Now, who could delegate and grant such extraordinary jurisdiction to each of the Apostles before their voluntary dispersion to the four parts of the earth? Who, but he to whom singly and separately Christ had given the plenitude of authority by making him the foundation of the Apostolic college, the Confirmer of the Apostolic body, the supreme Shepherd of all the Apostles as well as of the rest of the universal Church: Matt. 16. 18, 19; Luke 22. 32; John 21. 17.

(g) The extraordinary jurisdiction of each Apostle, being not only limited and temporary but simply delegated, was therefore untransmissible of its nature, or per se. It died a natural death and ceased altogether with the temporary necessities that gave rise to it, i. e. with the last of the Apostles.

Peter's jurisdiction, being ordinary or inherent in his office, is and must needs be as transmissible as the office to which it essentially belongs.

The theory that every Apostle had universal jurisdiction is indefensible. Even the partisans of the theory acknowledge with all Catholic theologians that, excepting Peter alone, none of the Apostles had, either collectively or individually, any authority whatever over one another, and much less over the entire Apostolic body. Such an acknowledgment is a plain confession that the jurisdiction of the other Apostles was not universal, since it did not include the noblest part of the Church—her Apostolic princes and rulers—who, by Divine appointment, recognised Peter alone as their visible superior and sovereign ruler.

Why does the successor of Peter receive the plenitude of jurisdiction immediately from Jesus Christ Himself?

Because neither the bishops nor the priests—collectively or individually—nor the whole Church, ever received the pontifical power granted to Peter and his successors exclusively (ibid.).—They cannot therefore communicate that which they have not, i. e. the pontifical sovereignty; nor can any one else on earth. There remains but one alternative: either Peter never had any successor, the pledge of Christ to the contrary notwithstanding (Matt. 16. 18 etc.)—or the successor of Peter, like Peter himself, receives his sovereign investiture immediately from Jesus Christ, who promised to perpetuate the Petrine office despite all the hostile powers or "gates of hell." (Ibid.)

Why do the bishops receive jurisdiction immediately from the Vicar of Jesus Christ?

Because our Lord made Peter the principle and bond of Apostolic unity, and therefore ordained that his bishops should receive jurisdiction not by consecration but by appointment—which of course can only come from a superior, and consequently from the Vicar of Christ on earth.

How do we know that the bishops do not receive jurisdiction by means of consecration or ordination, together with the fulness of the sacrament of Order, but by appointment from the Holy See?

From the words and actions of our Lord: for, by appointment exclusively did he confer jurisdiction on the Apostles both before and after their ordination and quite independently of it—thereby teaching (a) that jurisdiction is not conferred by the sacrament of Order but by appointment—and (b) that it may be conferred on men not vested with the clerical dignity, i. e. on the laity—even as it may be withheld from those vested with the episcopal character, as it was from the Apostles from the day of their ordination (Matt. 21. 26) to the eve of the Ascension (Matt. 28. 18): it being thoroughly distinct and separable from the priestly power of Order.

Comparative powers of the Pope and of the bishops

(a) As regards the power of Order, the bishops are the equals of the pope: sacerdotally, he is a bishop and so are they; they, as well as he, have received the plenitude of the priesthood.

But they are his inferiors and his subjects in the domain of jurisdiction and of the magisterial power. One man on earth may, but intermittently and for a few minutes only, justly exercise authority over the Vicar of Jesus Christ—namely, the pope's confessor when hearing the august penitent's confession.

(b) The Holy Father receives his jurisdiction directly from Jesus Christ at the instant he accepts the papal office, after his canonical election.

The bishops receive their jurisdiction immediately from the Vicar of Christ, the visible head of the Church.

(c) The jurisdiction of the Holy Father is universal and Church-wide; the jurisdiction of the bishops is local and restricted to their diocese or to the sphere allotted to them by the Vicar of Jesus Christ.

(d) The jurisdiction of the Holy Father is supreme and independent; the jurisdiction of the bishops subordinate and dependent on the authority of the pope.

(e) The pope is above purely human laws, civil and ecclesiastical—above the whole body of the Church universal; bishops are subject to the Holy Father and to all the laws and councils of the Church. In their relations with the sovereign Pontiff, they belong to the Church Governed, not to the Church Governing.

(f) The pope alone is the infallible teacher of the Church ex-cathedra, i. e. from the magisterial Chair of Peter.

Every other bishop is individually fallible, and in his relations with the successor of Peter, every bishop belongs to the Church Taught, not to the Church Teaching.

The whole episcopal body acting jointly with the visible head of the Church partakes of the infallibility of the Christ-appointed head, and is infallible by virtue of Christ's solemn promise to Peter: Luke 22. 32.

NOTE XXII

How can it be known that the extraordinary jurisdiction and the personal infallibility of each of the Apostles do not endure in their successors?

Answer:—From the testimony of Holy Scripture and the irrefragable witness of history.

We gather from Holy Writ that Titus, bishop of Crete (Tit. 1. 5) and Timothy, bishop of Ephesus (Tim. 1. 3), and the other bishops appointed by the Apostles (1 Pet. 5. 2; Apoc. 2. 1, 8, 12, 18),—v. g. the bishops of Smyrna, Pergamus, Thyatira—possessed nothing more than the local and ordinary jurisdiction enjoyed by bishops nowadays in their respective dioceses.

History knows of no bishops, except the successors of St. Peter, that ever claimed universal jurisdiction over the Church. Not even Photius, or Cerularius, or any of their schismatic successors, ever dared to claim authority over the holy Roman Church. Even now, Eastern schismatics recognise the Pope as *the first* Patriarch of the Church.

That the Apostles themselves did not regard the bishops consecrated by them as endowed, individually, with magisterial infallibility, seems evident from St. Paul's address to the Church officials whom he distinctly calls "bishops" (Acts 20. 28), and whom he summoned from Ephesus to Miletus. For, he predicts that some of them will fall into schism and heresy.

"Of your own selves," says he, "shall arise men speaking perverse things to draw away disciples after them" (Acts 20. 30). He puts the bishop of Ephesus, Timothy, on his guard against possible errors of doctrine as follows: "Avoid foolish and old wives' fables .... till I come attend to reading, to exhortation and to *doctrine* (1. Tim. 4. 7, 13),—"Avoid foolish and unlearned questions" (2. Tim. 2. 23).

He gives the same warning to the bishop of Crete, Titus, to whom he writes: "In all things show thyself an example of good work, in *doctrine*, in integrity, in gravity" (Tit. 2. 7)—"Avoid foolish questions" (Tit. 3. 9).

History attests that, from the death of the last Apostle to this 20th century, never have the bishops of the Church of God arrogated to themselves the special Apostolic prerogative of individual infallibility. The only infallible personality they ever recognised is that of the Christ-appointed Confirmer of the Faith (Luke 22. 32), Peter the Rock, ever living in his successors (Matt. 16. 18., etc.), viz., the bishop of Rome (1 Pet. 5. 13)—the "Babylon" from which Peter dates his first Epistle. "Babylon, that is to say, heathen persecuting Rome, as the Sibylline books of Jewish origin had long ago named it', observes Dr. Barry, (Papal Monarchy, p. 18).

The most overwhelming proof that the individual infallibility of every bishop is not essential to the preservation of the deposit of the Faith, is the fact that the Church has been doing without such a supererogatory gift for 1900 years without deviating by one single line from the path of revealed truth. Therefore, the experience of nineteen centuries proves that the three divine weapons of (a) continuous Tradition and (b) of close communion with the infallible Confirmer of the Faith together with (c) the corporate infallibility of the episcopate under its visible head—have abundantly sufficed to keep the Church from error.

Contrariwise, the extraordinary privilege of invidual infallibility was a morally imperative necessity as regards the twelve very first introducers of Christianity to the world. For, had the very first seed sown into the virgin soil of the Church been the cockle of false doctrine, error would have claimed the right of the first occupant, and the resultant evil had been irremediable by reason of the boundless faith reposed in the Apostles. No subsequent missionary efforts could have repaired the harm done. Nay, such efforts would have been repulsed with scorn by the disciples of the Apostles, who would have plausibly replied: "We would rather believe the Apostles, sent directly by the Saviour in person, than strangers and innovators."

Thus it would have come to pass that, the vaster the prestige of the Apostles, the more invincible the tenacity of their followers to cling to the Apostolic errors preached to them from the very start.

NOTE XXIII

Comparative Church-powers of Christ and of Peter

(First)—The threefold power of Christ as King, Prophet, and Priest, belongs to Him by right of nature and of absolute domain over all creation; whilst it belongs to Peter by grace of participation only, and through the infinite mercy of the Saviour.

(Second)—The universality of Christ's threefold power is absolute and infinite; whilst the universality, or rather the plenitude, of Peter's power is merely relative, i. e. it covers the entire sphere allotted to the whole Church—but that sphere itself is limited, as we shall proceed to show.

(1) Christ's Kingship is infinite. Peter's authority is circumscribed by the law of God and by the constitution of the Church as determined by her Lord and Master. Consequently, (a) Peter, or the Pope, cannot change the form of Church government—v. g. substitute autocracy for the Divine monarchy established by our Lord; (b) he cannot alter the order of the hierarchy—v. g. substitute priests or laymen for bishops in the ordinary and permanent administration of the Church; (c) he cannot create a new Church; (d) he cannot abrogate the existent Church, as Christ did the Synagogue.

(2) Christ's infallibility as Prophet or Teacher is absolute and infinite, not limited to questions of Faith and morals; it is inseparable from his Person and from his every act and utterance.

Peter's infallibility is limited to the public exercise of his office and is circumscribed by the deposit of Revelation, i. e. by both the written and the unwritten Word of God, by Holy Writ and by Divine tradition.

Consequently, (a) the pope cannot reveal new truths, (b) he cannot affix a new meaning to the Word of God; (c) he cannot set aside the New Testament or Divine tradition, or replace the law of Christ by a new law of his own device.

Besides, he may err as a private individual, and is infallible only as a public person teaching officially the whole Church in matters of Faith (Matt. 28. 19. etc.), and of morals (Matt. 16. 15 etc.) i. e. as to what God requires us to believe and to do to be acceptable to his divine Majesty.

(3) Christ's power as the High Priest of the Most High is causative and infinite.

Peter's sacerdotal power is not causative but instrumental, and is circumscribed by the seven Sacraments, or channels of grace, instituted by our Lord.

Consequently, (a) Peter, or the pope, cannot add to the number of the sacraments; (b) he cannot subtract therefrom; (c) he cannot alter their form; (d) he cannot change the matter thereof; (e) he cannot change their nature, v. g. turn the sacraments of the living into sacraments of the dead, and vice versa; (f) he cannot modify their character, whether delible or indelible; (g) still less can he abolish them, or any of them, altogether.

But Christ could at will effect the above and countless other additions, subtractions, or changes—or suppress all the sacraments without exception, by enabling human nature to do away with its inborn need of, and craving for, a sacramental system.

Falsely therefore is the Church accused of putting Peter above our Lord Himself. On the contrary, she declares Peter infinitely beneath the Master, not only as priest and prophet and king, but particularly as the foundation of the Church. When non-Catholics charge the Church with substituting Peter for Christ as the Rock whereon she is built, they know not whereof they speak and ignore her most notorious doctrine, which the sweet genius of St. Francis de Sales summarises with forceful lucidity.

We transpose and arrange the various paragraphs and sentences of our quotation from the Saint, so as to present a parallel tableau of the prerogatives of Christ and Peter and their office as Foundation of the Church.

First difference: our Lord is Foundation and Founder; St. Peter is foundation, not founder.

Second difference: Christ is the Foundation without other foundation; Peter is foundation, but founded on another Foundation, which is our blessed Lord Himself.

Third difference: Christ is the Foundation of the Natural, Mosaic, and Evangelic Church; Peter is the foundation of the Evangelic Church alone.

Fourth difference: Christ is Foundation perpetual and immortal; Peter is foundation subject to succession.

Fifth difference: Christ is Foundation of the Militant and Triumphant Church; Peter is foundation of the Militant not of the Triumphant Church.

Sixth difference: Christ is Foundation by His own nature; Peter is foundation by participation—ministerial, not absolute foundation—in short, administrator, not Lord.

Seventh difference: Christ is the Foundation of our faith, hope and charity—and of the efficacy of the sacraments. Peter is in no way the foundation of our faith, hope, and charity—nor of the efficacy of the Sacraments. (St. Francis de Sales: Cath. Controversy, Eng. tr., p. 246.)

NOTE XXIV

The alternative: either Peter or atheism

The ablest thinkers in the allied camps of Rationalism and Protestantism frankly acknowledge that whoever can delve deep down to the very bedrock of the Religious question—must face, at the bottom of it all, the following alternative: either there is no Divine revelation, or the Catholic Church, the Church of Peter, is in possession of it.

In four brief words: either Peter or atheism.

The argument is without a flaw.

They say: a revelation intrusted to a depository liable to falsify or misapprehend, or mistranslate, its meaning —would be of no practical use, and therefore unworthy the infinite wisdom of a Divine revelator.

Consequently, either there is no Revelation at all, or it has been intrusted to a medium of *infallible reliability*—i. e. to an infallible interpreter.

But the Catholic Church alone claims to be such an infallible interpreter of Revelation. Therefore, if the Catholic Church is false, there is no divine Revelation; and if there is no divine Revelation there is no Providence caring for and watching over the welfare of man; and if there is no Providence there is no God.

For, if the unsilenceable clamor of the soul for a Divine positive reply to the Whence and the Whether and the Wherefore—must remain without a Divine positive assurance, which assurance *alone* can make life worth living—then there is no Providence; and if there is no Providence there is no God, i. e. no Supremely Good Being overruling the destinies of mankind. So that, in the last analysis, as acknowledged nowadays by thinking Rationalists and Protestants, if Catholicity is not a Divine religion or revelation, then there is no Revelation whatsoever. If there is no Revelation there is no Providence; if there is no Providence there is no God.

We recapitulate the substance of the argument used by Protestant and rationalist thinkers: No Catholicity, logically means no Revelation. No Revelation, logically means no Providence. No Providence, logically means no God.

Therefore, no Catholicity, logically means Atheism.

Therefore, human reason, in its ultimate findings, is confronted with this alternative: either Catholicism or atheism. Either Peter, the Rock—or intellectual, moral and social anarchy, ending in Despair.

The subtlest genius England ever produced, John Henry Newman, had already, even *before* joining the Catholic Church, reached this inexorable conclusion—which is gradually burning its inexorable logic into the acutest minds of the age, and is visibly beginning to divide the civilized world, on the subject of Religion, into two distinct camps, and two only, viz., Catholics and Atheists.

The famous author of "Is Life Worth Living," W. H. Mallock, writes:

"The reality of supernatural religion being granted, the Roman Church alone of all the churches gives to

such a Religion a logical and organically coherent form."
(Mallock's reply to Father Fallon's note of inquiry,
dated January 23, 1899.)

Put in syllogistic form, Mr. Mallock's argument
is as follows:

If there exists a "supernatural religion," it must
necessarily be embodied in a rational or "logical form"
worthy of such a supernatural boon; but its only
"logical form" is "the Roman Church *alone* of all the
churches"—therefore, outside "the Roman Church,"
there is no supernatural religion, no Divine revelation.

The admission of a very influential Protestant
journal, the Christian Register, is still more emphatic:
It begins by asking, "Is any religion given by divine
revelation and supernatural authority? If so, which
Religion has been so given, what are its credentials
and what is its authority?"

The crucial query is answered in the following
pithy sentence: "When it comes to the final test
there is no escape from the most extreme position of
the Catholic Church or a total rejection of it."

That is to say: either there is no revealed Religion,
or that Religion, says the Register, must be "the
Catholic Church"—since, says the same witness, it
must be both infallible and sovereign, and the Catholic
Church alone of all the churches claims to be infallible in her teaching and sovereign in her authority.

"Revealed Religion," says the Register, "is infallible
if God knows the truth and knows how to tell
it." Therefore, even according to the Register, to
deny the infallibility of revealed Religion is to blas-
pheme against the Omniscience and Wisdom of God
the Revealer.

Of the sovereign authority inherent in such a Revealed Religion, the Register writes: "A Religion given by supernatural authority is not to be neglected or resisted. *It has the right to command the alligiance of every human being.* Outside of this Religion there is no truth that can be set over against it, and beyond its jurisdiction no human being has the right to live, or, living, to choose his own course of action." (Quoted by the N. Y. Freeman's Journal, March 29, 1902—Italics ours.)

The logical conclusion of the Protestant organ is that, either there is no revealed Religion at all, or "there is no escape from the most extreme position of the Catholic Church."

Now, what Protestants and all non-Catholics regard as "the most extreme position of the Catholic Church" is her magisterial infallibility and her sovereign authority—both summed up in Peter.

Therefore, according to non-Catholic *thinkers,* "there is no escape" from Papal infallibility and soveeignty: either Peter or atheism.

The indefectibility of the Rock is the crowning glory of its Creator, Jesus the Christ.

But does not papal infallibility, as well as papal sovereignity, detract from the honor due to God?

Not a tittle more than the divine foresight of the Prophets or the inspiration of the sacred writers of the Word of God.

The reverse is the truth.

All those miraculous gifts—prophecy, inspiration, infallibility etc.—add immeasurably to the *external* glory of God. For, the more intensively and extensively does the Creator reflect His attributes in His creature, the more beautifully is He Himself honored, exalted, and glorified in His own works.

They do not understand the a, b, c of the redemptive Plan of God who have yet to learn that the Redeemer's aim is to restore and honor the erstwhile degraded prey of Satan and his hosts, viz., *poor fallen man and the entire lower creation,* affected by the original fall. Hence God's particular delight in loading man with honors divine, and in partly raising His lower creation itself to the supernatural order by using it in the sacraments and in the sacramentals of His Church—v. g. water, wine, olive oil, balsam, incense, wheaten bread, salt, beeswax, the snow-white fleece of spotless lambs, altar-stones, cedar or other wood used in the construction of her tabernacles and of her temples, etc. etc.

This is but an earnest of the full and glorious restoration that awaits man and all the lower kingdoms of nature at the expiration of the Christian Cycle of Time—a restoration for which St. Paul assures us "the whole creation groaneth": Ro. 8. 22.

Nor must it be forgotten that all those divine gifts, offices, prerogatives—prophecy, inspiration, infallibility, divine authority, etc. are not vouchsafed for the mere glorification of their recipients but for the benefit of all mankind. They are the *means* to an end. Now, *the end is greater than the means and is within the reach of all men,* to wit: that they become, here below, really "partakers of the Divine nature" (2 Pet. 1. 4)—men-gods as Christ is God-man—that they be raised to a higher order of creatures, a strictly divine order of being as far above human nature as the human is above the brute creation.

Such a deified state, open as it is to all "men of good will" (Luke 2. 14), is intrinsically above all the offices and the sacraments used as means thereunto—not excepting the sacramental power of consecration; for this may be exercised by one in a state of sin, whilst, on the other hand, the Godhead so dwells in man deified by sanctifying grace that God and the human soul really draw the same Breath of Divine life—breathing simultaneously out of the same Breath—namely, the Adorable Breath of God known and adored as the thrice Holy Spirit.

It is, then, in perfect keeping with the Divine Plan that the selfsame God who willed that we all, without exception, "should be called and should be *verily the sons of God*" (1 John 3. 1) for the greater glory of God and of man—it is, we repeat, in perfect-keeping with the Plan of God Incarnate that He should also will to exercise His own Priesthood through the ministry of man, and should likewise will to exercise His Headship over His Body through the same human agency.

Thus God Incarnate who, *for our sake,* delegated to His Apostles His own power to forgive sin (John 20. 23), has likewise, out of love *for us all,* delegated to Peter—in so far as He made him the Rock by grace and participation—His own indefectibility as the eternal and divine Rock by nature.

Thus it is that papal infallibility, as well as papal sovereignty, redounds to the eternal glory of God and to the greatest honor and welfare of mankind.

Conclusion

In this and in a previous work, we have seen that Peter's divine name is his Divine credential, by reason of its divine bestowal, import, and treatment in Holy Writ.

Now, this Divine credential and title of office occurs one hundred and sixty six times in the New Testament. And oh how eloquently do these 166 iterations of the Petrine name speak to the eye and to the ear!

To the eye of the faithful reader, they show forth one hundred and sixty-six Christ-signed proclamations of the Petrine office—signed and written by the hand of God on as many plates of gold, and adorning the length and height and breadth of the inner and outer walls of the scriptural Temple.

To the ear of the faithful hearer, these 166 iterations of the Petrine name sound like one hundred and sixty-six silver trumpets encircling the dome of the grand Temple, and blown by the mouth of the Angel of the Covenant, and thrilling all the stones of the Temple, with the "Tu es Petrus" intoned by the Saviour, nineteen centuries ago.

J H V H

Imprimi potest:

A. Heuchemer, V. G.

January 18 A. D. 1909

San Antonio, Texas

From Saint Pius X Press

Title	Price
Bernadette of Lourdes	25.00
Characteristics of True Devotion	12.00
Conference Matter For Religious	25.00
Eternal Punishment	15.00
Holiness Of Life	15.00
Holy Week Manual For Servers	15.00
Readings For Each Sunday In The Year	12.95
Spiritual Maxims	18.00
The Divine Office	15.00
The Mirror of the Blessed Virgin Mary and The Psalter of Our Lady	25.00
The Present Crisis of the Holy See	15.00
The Religious State	11.95
Vocations	9.95
New Lights On Pastoral Problems	15.00
Peter's Name	15.00
The Virtues Of A Religious Superior	15.00
Practical Method of Reading the Breviary	20.00
The Cult of Our Lady	15.00
The Possibility of Invincible Ignorance of the Natural Law	30.00

Saint Pius X Press

Box 74
Delia KS 66418
www.stpiusxpress.com

If you have a book that you are looking for to be reprinted and we do not have it listed, contact us at contact@stpiusxpress.com

Made in the USA
Lexington, KY
02 August 2014